THE MOTHER OF THE LORD

THE MOTHER OF THE LORD
Memory, Presence, Hope

THE PONTIFICAL INTERNATIONAL MARIAN ACADEMY

Presenting a Review of the
Actual Questions Facing Mariology Today

ST PAULS

Translator of the Text: Thomas A. Thompson, S.M.
Secretarial Assistance: Sr. M. Jean Frisk

Library of Congress Cataloging-in-Publication Data

[Madre dell Signore. English]
The Mother of the Lord : memory, presence, hope.
    p. cm.
Letter of the Pontifical International Marian Academy, dated December 8, 2000.
Includes bibliographical references.
ISBN 978-0-8189-1249-8
1. Mary, Blessed Virgin, Saint—Theology.   I. Pontifical International Marian
Academy.   II. Title.

BT613.M28713   2007
232.91—dc22

                                        2007006753

Produced and designed in the United States of America by the
Fathers and Brothers of the Society of St. Paul,
2187 Victory Boulevard, Staten Island, New York 10314-6603
as part of their communications apostolate.

ISBN 13: 978-0-8189-1249-8
ISBN 10: 0-8189-1249-9

Printing Information:

Current Printing - first digit	1	2	3	4	5	6	7	8	9	10

Year of Current Printing - first year shown

2007	2008	2009	2010	2011	2012	2013	2014	2015	2016

TABLE OF CONTENTS

PREFACE TO THE FRENCH EDITION

This text is offered by the Pontifical International Marian Academy to those who wish to reflect on and study in a systematic way the person and mission of the Blessed Virgin Mary. It is presented as a "letter" providing an outline of the elements comprised in Mariology, references to the Church's teaching on these topics, and finally, a discussion of the Marian questions currently investigated, discussed, and debated. The letter suggests ways in which a greater consciousness of the Marian truths can lead to a deeper appreciation of the marvelous work which the Holy Trinity has accomplished in Mary for the sake of all humanity. Also, the letter wishes to promote dialogue on how the Marian teachings can be presented in new and varied cultural settings.

After the introduction, which attempts to describe the theological and cultural context at the beginning of Christianity's third millennium, the letter has three sections.

The first section provides suggestions for approaching Marian questions in a positive and profitable way. Research dealing with Marian topics is especially suited for interdisciplinary studies involving other fields of theological inquiry.

The second section shows the challenges which must be met so that reflection on the Virgin Mary may enter the heart and the mind of individuals and, through them, may influence daily life and conduct.

The last section deals with prayer in the spirit of Mary and the role that the Virgin Mary has in the Church's liturgy and devotional life.

My wish is that these pages may help you to come to a deeper knowledge of the true identity of the Virgin Mary, Mother of God and Mother of the Church.

Vincent Battaglia, OFM
Pontifical International Marian Academy

PREFACE TO THE ITALIAN EDITION

This document was originally written in preparation for the Twentieth Mariological and Marian Congress which was held in Rome, September 14-25, 2000. As the first congress of Christianity's third millennium, it appeared an opportune moment for the Pontifical International Marian Academy to survey various mariological and Marian societies on the actual questions which are facing Marian devotion and the manner in which Marian theological reflection is conducted. The Holy See, to which the Pontifical Academy renders its service, was informed of this project and offered its encouragement, as a way of fulfilling its mission "to coordinate the cooperation of all the societies and faculties which have as their purpose to promote devotion to Mary" (John XXIII, *Maiora in dies*). As a document coming from a Pontifical Academy, the sources will be the writings of the great teachers of the Church, the texts of the liturgy, the ecumenical councils, the various dicasteries and commissions of the Holy See, and episcopal conferences. Far from proposing a type of "Marian Denzinger," the letter is conscious of the many contributions coming from individual theologians. This document was reviewed by some Marian societies, many of which sent their suggestions.

This document is issued in the name of the Pontifical International Marian Academy, in the confident hope that it will contribute to and help clarify several questions on Marian studies, offer suggestions for future developments, and indicate several challenges, which, in the opinion of the Pontifical

Academy, face Marian devotion at the beginning of this new millennium.

This document wishes above all to be a humble expression of filial devotion of the Pontifical Academy to the Mother of God and our Mother, and sign of friendship to the many who labor with joyful dedication in the task of theological reflection on Mary, the luminous icon of the Trinity.

Gaspar Calvo Moralejo, OFM
Stefano Cecchin, OFM

INTRODUCTION

The Historical-cultural Context
at the Beginning of the Third Millennium

1. The passage from Christianity's second to the third millennium is for the theologian and the student of mariology an opportune moment to reflect upon, in the light of faith, the contemporary situation of humanity and the Church, to review the recent past, and, as we examine the signs of the times (cf. Mt 16:3), to discern some directions and orientations for the future.

To accomplish the task, the theologian would do well to take on the attitude of the Virgin Mary, who in her heart kept the words and the actions of her Son and sought to understand them through remembrance, through dialogue, and through prayerful pondering (cf. Lk 2:19, 51).

Such reflection should lead theologians not only to acknowledge the past errors of individuals and of civil and religious institutions, but also to find a new path which they themselves can confidently and resolutely follow and, by their example, propose to believers.

Reasons for Concern

2. If theologians wish that their message be taken seriously, they should examine contemporary culture, both its light and dark sides. Some matters for concern immediately arise.

So many men and women have crossed the threshold to

the new millennium burdened with the sadness of delusion and frustration. They are weighed down by remembrance of inhuman and destructive dictatorships, by the scars from two world wars, by images from concentration camps. They know that the hatreds of the past have not been resolved nor have the sources for discord been eliminated.

Although great progress has been made, there are still gross inequalities. The divide between the rich and the poor has increased. External debts, which especially burden countries of the Third World and produce tragic consequences (starvation, death from diseases which can be prevented, and high rates of illiteracy) have increased.

Ecologically, we can see the consequences of the disorders caused by "the lack *of due respect for nature"* and from "the plundering of natural resources."[1] Deserts have increased due to the destruction of forests and the pollution of the water, the air, and the soil. Some now speak of the *suffering of the earth* to describe the irreparable harm inflicted on nature. They denounce the attacks on the aesthetic dimensions of creation. Populations live in anguished concern for the future of our planet. John Paul II has said that the present ecological crisis presents a grave moral problem.[2]

In the ethical and social areas, the concerns are many. The culture of death — symbolized in capital punishment which still exists in many countries — has tragic consequences: widespread attacks against life in its initial and terminal stages, fratricidal and racial rivalries, displacement of populations, genocide, ethnic cleansing, terrorism and violence, death squads. Other concerns are the immoderate search for wealth and the assumption that hedonism is an acceptable lifestyle; the weakening of the

---

[1] John Paul II, *Peace with God the Creator, Peace with All of Creation,* Message for the Celebration of the World Day of Peace 1990 (8 December 1990), 1, in *AAS* 82 (1990), 147; in *OR* (18-26 December 1989), 1.

[2] Cf. *Ibid.*, 6-7, 150-151.

family structure; the high rate of unemployment; the influx of immigrants in large numbers; indignities committed against women who are subjected to new forms of slavery; the growing use of drugs threatening health; the misery and degradation in which whole populations find themselves. Especially lamentable is the violence inflicted on children: soldier-children, street children, children forced to work in inhuman conditions with long hours and little compensation, children who are used to satisfy adults' pleasure and forced into the nefarious market of human organs.

Signs of Hope

3. But the signs of hope are not absent. For theologians and students of mariology, the supreme sign of hope is the resurrected Christ, "For in him all the fulness was pleased to dwell, and through him [Christ] to reconcile all things for him, making peace by the blood of his cross [through him], whether those on earth or those in heaven" (Col 1:19-20). Mary's Assumption is a sign of hope.[3] She is the mother of Jesus (cf. Jn 14:6), and mother of the living (cf. Gen 3:20). But, founded on the word of God (cf. Mt 28:20; Jn 16:33) and recognized by faith alone, beyond these signs, there are other developments in our world perceived by the attentive observer. From modernity's individualistic model, a new model is perceptible, one which involves *relationships, solidarity, cooperation* and *complementarity* — all elements which respect the order of nature and which are in perfect harmony with the Gospel teaching. Some maintain that there is a clear need for collective responsibility to replace *competitive globalization* with *cooperative globalization*, the exploitation of

---

[3] *LG* 68; Also in *Mother of Christ, Mother of the Church: Documents on the Blessed Virgin Mary* (hereafter *MOC*), Pauline Books & Media, 2001, 82.

persons and of nature with a respectful and communal *reciprocity*, the search for the individual's well-being with the striving for the *common good* and for *peace*, the search for possessions with the willingness to give freely and demand nothing in return.

Insertion in the Actual Historical-cultural Context

4. In this period of great change, it is necessary that theologians, students of mariology, and those who welcome Mary into their lives as the inestimable gift of the crucified Christ (cf. Jn 19:25-27) become part of our world's actual historical-cultural setting, and, following the example of the Mother of the Lord, choose the values of life, of solidarity and service, for promoting and advancing a "civilization of love."

In particular the phenomena of globalization requires that mariology overcome every tendency toward isolation and that it be inserted, while preserving its proper identity, in the context of contemporary culture and in the emerging theological developments — all within the horizon of the history of salvation which ever progresses.

Also the ability to relate, an intrinsic quality of the human person, invites us to value the vast network of relations by which the Blessed Virgin Mary is related to the Most Holy Trinity, to the Church, to humanity, to the world: she is a "totally relational" creature. From these considerations, a clear direction is evident: There is a future for a mariology which, rooted in the experience of faith, gives a word of hope and a clarifying response to the specific questions which trouble human relationships and obscure the saving mission of the Church.

5. In this time of transition, it would be well to examine mariology's recent past. By that we mean the period from 1964, the year of the promulgation of the constitution *Lumen Gentium* (21 November 1964), to 2000, the Year of Jubilee commemorating the second millennium of the birth of the Savior. The pontificate of Pius XII (1939-1958), during which the dogmatic definition of the Assumption of Mary (1 November 1950)[4] occurred, is especially significant. The mariology of those years, designated in an abbreviated way as a "mariology of privileges," reached its climax. Also present in the vast mariological production of those years was, sometimes incipiently and other times openly, a dangerous maximalism, both in theological proposals and in expressions of devotion.

Mariology Seen in the Perspective of Salvation History

6. On 21 November 1964, Vatican II promulgated the dogmatic constitution *Lumen Gentium*, with its eighth chapter dedicated to the teaching on "The Blessed Virgin Mary, Mother of God, in the Mystery of Christ and the Church." This chapter, through its fidelity to tradition, its openness to new circumstances, and its balancing of different positions, is not only of great magisterial value, but also a doctrinal masterpiece on the Mother of the Lord.[5] Here we wish to comment on two points: the placement of the Marian teaching in the perspective of salvation history

---

4   Text in *AAS* 42 (1950), 753-773; *MOC*, 31.

5   "…this session has ended with an incomparable hymn in praise of the Virgin Mother of God. For this is the first time… that any ecumenical council has stated the Catholic doctrine on the place that should be accorded to the Blessed Virgin Mary in the mystery of Christ and of the Church" (Paul VI, *Discourse at the Close of the Third Session of the Second Vatican Ecumenical Council* (hereafter *Discourse at the Close of the Third Session*), 22 November 1964, in *AAS* 56 (1964), 1014; *OR* (Italian ed.; 22 November 1964).

and its insertion into the context of the mystery of Christ and of the Church.

The first signals the end of the long use of the deductive method in theological reflection on the Virgin Mary so as to view her within the history of salvation, within the Sacred Scriptures, and within the commentaries of the early Christian writers. The second eliminates the risk that mariology become enclosed on itself and isolated from the general context of theology.

Mariology Seen in Anthropological Perspective

7. The "anthropological turn" of theology has its repercussions in mariology. The apostolic exhortation *Marialis Cultus,* of Paul VI (2 February 1974), was the document which, together with contemporary developments, especially the aspirations of women searching new avenues of responsibility in the various areas of life, presented to mariology the need for this anthropological turn. *Marialis Cultus,* with the certainty based on the experience of faith, presents Mary as the response to contemporary anthropological aspirations:

> Contemplated in the episodes of the Gospels and in the reality which she already possesses in the City of God, the Blessed Virgin Mary offers a calm vision and a reassuring word to modern man, torn as he often is between anguish and hope, defeated by the sense of his own limitations and assailed by limitless aspirations, troubled in his mind and divided in his heart, uncertain before the riddle of death, oppressed by loneliness while yearning for fellowship, a prey to boredom and disgust. She shows forth the victory of hope over anguish, of fellowship over solitude, of peace over anxiety, of joy and beauty over boredom

and disgust, of eternal visions over earthly ones, of life over death.[6]

Renewal, Reclaiming, Inculturation

8. After Vatican II, students of mariology pursued a triple course of renewal, reclaiming, and inculturation. Thus, to give some examples:

— post-conciliar Marian theology has investigated the profound relation of Mary to the Holy Spirit;

— it has reviewed the fundamental points of doctrinal mariology — the divine and virginal maternity, the Immaculate Conception, Mary's cooperation in the work of salvation, the Assumption — with the purpose of gaining understanding of the way these doctrines can be related to the contemporary situation;

— it has studied the role of Mary in the history of evangelization and her place in the theology of liberation;

— it has elevated popular Marian devotion and has made its relation to the liturgy clearer;

— it has seen the image of the *tota pulchra*, "splendor of the Church," as a key point of theological aesthetics;

---

[6] Paul VI, Apostolic Exhortation *Marialis Cultus* (*MC*), 57, in *AAS* 66 (1974), 113-168; in *MOC*, 127: "In the convergence of the data of faith and the data of the anthropological sciences, when these turn their attention to Mary of Nazareth, one understands more clearly that the Virgin is both the highest historical realization of the Gospel and the woman who, through her self-control, her sense of responsibility, her openness to others and to the spirit of service, her strength and her love, is the most completely realized on the human level. For example, the necessity has been noted: of drawing out the relevance of the human reality of the Virgin to people in our own time, stressing the fact that she is an historical person, a humble Jewish girl; of showing forth the permanent and universal human values of Mary in such a way that discourse about her throws light on discourse about man." (Congregation for Catholic Education, Circular Letter *The Virgin Mary in Intellectual and Spiritual Formation* (*VMISF*), 25 March 1988, 15, in *MOC*, 339.

— it has well illustrated the action of Mary "living the life of the Spirit" as a disciple of Christ;

— it has accepted specific values from a feminist perspective to arrive at a greater understanding of "Mary, the woman of Nazareth";

— it has promoted an ecumenical dialogue on the Mother of the Lord, indispensable for a Church on the way to the unity wished by Jesus; it has developed comprehensive reflection on the relations between Judaism and Christianity in which is affirmed the continuity and the unity of the covenant through which it has shown that there is no true break between the old and the new testaments;

— it has begun an encounter with Islam and with the great historic religions of Asia (Buddhism, Hinduism, Taoism, Confucianism, Shintoism) in which Catholic theologians, faithful to the New Testament revelation, affirm on the one hand the unique and necessary salvific mediation of Christ,[7] and, on the other hand, have investigated the salvific possibility of other religions, which "must be situated in the context of the universal active presence of the Spirit of Christ."[8]

9. The second half of the twentieth century witnessed a renewed interest in *inculturation.* Vatican II, especially in the constitution *Gaudium et Spes* and in the decree *Ad Gentes* (both promulgated 7 December 1995), spoke of the urgency of the inculturation of the faith and presented some suggestions for this task. Also the synod of bishops of 1974, dedicated to evangelization, and the

---

[7]   Cf. Congregation for the Doctrine of the Faith, *Declaration on the Unicity and Salvific Universality of Jesus Christ and the Church. Dominus Jesus* (6 August 2000), in *AAS* 92 (2000), 742-765; in *OR* (6 September 2000).

[8]   International Theological Commission, *Christianity and the World Religions* (30 September 1996) 49, in *EV*, 623, no. 1037; *Origins* 27/10 (14 August 1997).

one of 1977, dedicated to catechetics, provided many helpful points on inculturation. From the 1974 synod of bishops there came Paul VI's *Evangelii Nuntiandi* (8 December 1975), and from the second synod came John Paul II's apostolic exhortation *Catechesi Tradendae* (16 October 1979).[9] The extraordinary synod of 1985, convoked to mark the twentieth anniversary of the conclusion of Vatican II, recalled the double aspect of inculturation: "the intimate transformation of authentic cultural values through their integration in Christianity and the implanting of Christian values in the various human cultures."[10] Also the Pontifical Biblical Commission and the Pontifical Theological Commission have devoted important and significant studies to questions related to the inculturation of faith,[11] as has the Congregation for Divine Worship and the Discipline of the Sacraments in its instruction, *Varietates Legitimae* (25 January 1994), in which specific indications are given for implanting the liturgy in different cultures.[12]

Because "the mystery of Incarnation of the Word was also a cultural incarnation,"[13] it can be easily seen that mariology

---

[9] Paul VI, Apostolic Exhortation *Evangelization in the Modern World. Evangelii Nuntiandi,* 20, 63, in *AAS* 68 (1976), 5-76; in *OR* (25 December 1975); John Paul II, Apostolic Exhortation *On Catechesis in Our Time. Catechesi Tradendae,* 53, in *AAS* 71 (1979), 1277-1340; in *OR* (12 November 1979).

[10] *The Church in the Word of God Celebrates the Mysteries of Christ for the Salvation of the World. Exeunte Coetu Secundo,* final relatio of the second extraordinary synod (7 December 1985), in *OR* (16 December 1985), 6-9.

[11] Cf. Pontifical Biblical Commission, *Fede e cultura alla luce della Bibbia — Foi et culture à la lumière de la Bible.* Torino, LDC, 1981; Pontifical Theological Commission, *Fede e inculturazione* (3-8 October 1988), in *EV* 11, 846-895, nos. 1347-1424.

[12] Congregation for Divine Worship and the Discipline of the Sacraments, Instruction *Varietates Legitimae — On Inculturation and the Roman Liturgy* (25 January 1994), in *AAS* 87 (1995), 288-314. This instruction refers frequently to John Paul II's Apostolic Letter *On the 25th Anniversary of the Constitution Sacrosanctum Concilium (SC). Vicesimus Quintus Annus* (4 December 1988); on inculturation see no. 16, in *AAS* 81 (1989), 897-918; in *OR* (22 May 1989), 9-10.

[13] John Paul II, *Discourse to University Professors and Men of Culture in Coimbra, Portugal, about the Improvement of Mankind and Cooperation among Peoples through Culture* (15 May 1982), in *OR* (5 July 1982), 6-7; in *Insegnamenti di Giovanni Paolo II (Insegnamenti),* V/2 (1982), 1695.

cannot remain apart from inculturation. In various regions — especially in Latin America — methods of inculturation of doctrine and of Marian devotion have been developed which are producing positive results. However, in other cases, cultural syncretism and doctrinal expressions which are not compatible with the Catholic faith have arisen. These results show how delicate is this process of inculturation, which requires much wisdom and prudence and, generally speaking, a period of maturation.

The Regionalization of Mariology

10. At the end of the twentieth century another phenomenon appeared: the "regionalization" of theology. From its Euro-centric phase, when the old continent had a virtual monoploy on "doing theology," new centers of theological study have developed on various continents. In North America, in addition to its traditional interest in biblical and ecumenical themes, were now added feminist theology and "practical" theology, for example, *black theology*. In Latin America, with the assistance of the episcopal conferences (Medellin 1968, Puebla 1979, Santo Domingo 1992), there arose liberation theology which pointed out that the situation of misery and of oppression which characterized many countries was a grievous offense against God. From this new consciousness, there was developed an integral theology which highlighted a liberating and energizing vision of life — a theology in which the memory of past centuries of oppression, the present situation of sorrow and struggle, the future signed with hope, together with progress on the way to earthly liberation — all are considered as a sign of the definitive eschatological liberation. In the context of such theology, the Mother of the Savior is recognized as "the most perfect image of freedom and

of the liberation of humanity and of the universe."[14]

There is great interest in developing a specifically African theology, free from the political overtones and the colonialism with which the preaching of the Gospel was associated from the sixteenth to the twentieth century. Such a theology, which is not a copy of western theology nor a simple adaptation of it, would enter deeply into the soul of the African people and express their reflection on Christian revelation in terms faithful to the *depositum fidei* and consonant with the centuries-old African culture. Such a theology, in the context of the countries of black Africa in where there is truly "anthropological poverty," would be a way of understanding God's salvific plan for the African peoples and a way for the further development and reclaiming the true identity of Africa.

Also a native theology is arising in Asia, a continent so varied and complex, where Christianity originated, but where it is nevertheless a religion of the minority in these large and densely populated lands. The task is similar to mining a huge vein in the mountain of revealed truths in order to claim the precious minerals of God's saving word. Such a theology, while faithful to the scriptural text, must be attentive to the vital context in which it is found, namely, one of oppressive poverty and of daily contact with the world's religions — the reality from which it cannot be separated. A theology which seeks to be authentically Asian must give careful attention to the immense patrimony of Asia's religious and spiritual nature and its proud cultural tradition, and must be free from dependence on western theology, which itself must be purified of inconsistencies and compromises.

---

[14] Congregation for the Doctrine of the Faith, *Instruction on Christian Freedom and Liberation. Libertatis conscientia* (22 March 1986), 97, in *AAS* 79 (1987), 554-599; in *OR* (7 April 1986) 1, 4.

11. Such is the theological and cultural context in which today's students of mariology confront their responsibility. In the Church and with the Church they should be conscious of the cultural ambiance in which they live and work and be in close contact with contemporary theology and its societal concerns.

They investigate the role of the Mother of Jesus in the history of salvation, always aware of the actual situation of contemporary men and women in whose lives salvation history continues.

They study the sources and reflect on the history, reflect on the fast-moving present, and discern the signs of the future — all so as to see the Virgin always united with the Savior, her Son, who continues, in her "eternal today" of glory, to be active in favor of people as they debate the meaning of events. They bless God because, in the power of the Spirit, he has glorified Christ raising him from the dead and has glorified the mother in the event of her Assumption. They do not evade the questions coming from many quarters asking what significance these events, which happened more than twenty centuries ago, have in a world in which death, injustice, and oppression dominate. They appreciate the great value of theology developed through the centuries, especially in Western Europe, but they understand that, at the beginning of the third millennium, the situation has changed. Peoples of the third world intensely participate in theological discourse with original insights. Women are acquiring the theological status which, because of historical circumstances, was previously denied them. Ecumenism and the interreligious dialogue require new attitudes for dealing with the traditional mariological themes.

Our Purpose

12. In the year of the great jubilee of the second millennium of the birth of Christ by the Virgin Mary, on the fiftieth anniversary of the doctrine of Mary's Assumption, defined by Pius XII on 1 November 1950, and on the first International Mariological-Marian Congress of the third millennium, it seemed appropriate for the Pontifical International Marian Academy to address this letter, as a friend, to the students of mariology and to pastoral ministers interested in Marian devotion, and to share with them some reflections on the actual situation and the contributions which mariology can make to the contemporary scene.

This letter is not intended to be comprehensive or authoritative. Among the many "mariological questions" — doctrinal and pastoral — discussed in our time, the Academy's council proposes a few themes that the Holy Father has addressed to theologians and pastoral ministers.

This letter is motivated by our love for the Virgin Mary, mother of our Lord Jesus Christ, by the service which the Pontifical Academy wishes to offer to the Holy See, by the common interests which we share with the various mariological societies, and by the friendship which bonds us to many students of mariology and to rectors of Marian shrines whose evident dedication to studying and promoting devotion to Mary is a source of no little joy and happiness for us.

ABBREVIATIONS

AAS	*Acta Apostolicae Sedis.*
BAC	*Biblioteca de Autores Cristianos.* Madrid, 1950.
CCCM	*Corpus Christianorum. Continuatio Mediaevalis.* Turnhout, 1966 seg.
CCL	*Corpus Christianorum. Series Latina,* Turnhout, 1953.
CSCO	*Corpus Scriptorum Christianorum Orientalium.* Paris/ Louvain, 1903.
CSEL	*Corpus Scriptorum Ecclesiasticorum Latinorum.* Vienna, 1866.
DS	H. Denzinger-A. Schönmetzer, *Enchiridion symbolorum, definitionum et declarationum de rebus fidei et morum.*
DACL	*Dictionnaire d'Archéologie chrétienne et de Liturgie.* Paris, 1907-1953.
EV	*Enchiridion Vaticanum. Documenti ufficiali del Concilio Vaticano II* (1962-65) *e della Santa Sede* (1966) Bologna, 1966.
MOC	*Mother of Christ, Mother of the Church: Documents on the Blessed Virgin Mary.* Pauline Books & Media, 2001.
MEERSSEMANN	*Der Hymnos Akathistos im Abendland.* Freiburg, I. 1958; II, 1960.
Monumenta OSM	*Monumenta Ordinis Servorum Sanctae Mariae.* A. Morini, P. Souliver, R. Taucci. Bruxelles, 1897-1937.
NBA	*Nuova Biblioteca Agostiniana.* Cattedra Agostiniana, Roma, 1965.
OR	*Osservatore Romano.* (English ed., unless otherwise noted).
ORIGINS	*CNS Documentary Service.*
PG	*Patrologia Graeca,* ed. J.P. Migne, Paris, 1857-1886.
PL	*Patrologia Latina,* ed. J.P. Migne, Paris, 1884.

SAEMO	*Sancti Ambrosii Episcopi Mediolanensis Opera.* Milan/ Rome, 1979.
SBO	*Sancti Bernardi Opera,* I-VIII, ed. by. J. Leclercq, C.H. Talbot, H.M. Rochais, Rome, 1957-77.
SCh	*Sources Chrétiennes,* Paris, 1941.
TMPM	*Testi Mariani del Primo Millennio,* 1-4, ed. O. Gharib, E.M. Toniolo, L. Gambero, O. DiNola, Roma, 1988-1991.
TPS	*The Pope Speaks.*

Resources for Marian Documents

Mary in the Church: A Selection of Teaching Documents. United States Conference of Catholic Bishops. Washington, DC, 2003.

Mother of Christ, Mother of the Church: Documents on the Blessed Virgin Mary. Introductions by M. Jean Frisk, S.T.L. General Editor: Marianne Lorraine Trouve. Boston: Pauline Books & Media, 2001.

Biblical Abbreviations

OLD TESTAMENT

Genesis	Gn	Nehemiah	Ne	Baruch	Ba
Exodus	Ex	Tobit	Tb	Ezekiel	Ezk
Leviticus	Lv	Judith	Jdt	Daniel	Dn
Numbers	Nb	Esther	Est	Hosea	Ho
Deuteronomy	Dt	1 Maccabees	1 M	Joel	Jl
Joshua	Jos	2 Maccabees	2 M	Amos	Am
Judges	Jg	Job	Jb	Obadiah	Ob
Ruth	Rt	Psalms	Ps	Jonah	Jon
1 Samuel	1 S	Proverbs	Pr	Micah	Mi
2 Samuel	2 S	Ecclesiastes	Ec	Nahum	Na
1 Kings	1 K	Song of Songs	Sg	Habakkuk	Hab
2 Kings	2 K	Wisdom	Ws	Zephaniah	Zp
1 Chronicles	1 Ch	Sirach	Si	Haggai	Hg
2 Chronicles	2 Ch	Isaiah	Is	Malachi	Ml
Ezra	Ezr	Jeremiah	Jr	Zechariah	Zc
		Lamentations	Lm		

NEW TESTAMENT

Matthew	Mt	Ephesians	Eph	Hebrews	Heb
Mark	Mk	Philippians	Ph	James	Jm
Luke	Lk	Colossians	Col	1 Peter	1 P
John	Jn	1 Thessalonians	1 Th	2 Peter	2 P
Acts	Ac	2 Thessalonians	2 Th	1 John	1 Jn
Romans	Rm	1 Timothy	1 Tm	2 John	2 Jn
1 Corinthians	1 Cor	2 Timothy	2 Tm	3 John	3 Jn
2 Corinthians	2 Cor	Titus	Tt	Jude	Jude
Galatians	Gal	Philemon	Phm	Revelation	Rv

I

FOR A CORRECT APPROACH TO THE MYSTERY OF THE MOTHER OF THE LORD

13. Mariology is a part of theology, a central component, because the Virgin Mary was intimately related to the events of our salvation: the Incarnation of the Word (cf. Lk 1:26-38; Mt 1:18-25); the manifestation of Jesus to the shepherds (cf. Lk 2:8-14) and to the magi (cf. Mt 2:9-10) who respectively were representatives of Jews and Gentiles; the manifestation of the Messiah in the Temple to Simeon and Anna (cf. Lk 2:22-38) and then at Cana of Galilee to the disciples at the beginning of Christ's public life (cf. Jn 2:1-12); the death of the Lord on the cross (cf. Jn 19:25-27); and the outpouring of the gift of the Spirit at Pentecost (cf. Ac 1:12-14; 2:1-4). From these events the relation of mariology to the other theological disciplines becomes apparent.

Christology and Mariology

14. Jesus, Son of God and "son of man," the Messiah and Savior, was born of Mary, flesh of her flesh; she conceived him, gave him birth, nourished him, and, together with Joseph her husband, educated him in the traditions of the Jewish people. She is the true mother of Jesus and so between her and her Son there exists an indissoluble, maternal-filial bond. The person and the mission of Jesus the Savior casts light on the figure of the mother, that is, Christology enlightens mariology. And, to a degree, mariology makes a contribution to Christology. Paul VI observed, the "knowledge of true Catholic doctrine on the Blessed Virgin Mary will always be an effective aid to proper understanding of the mystery of Christ and the Church."[15] "The Church, through Mary, that 'exceptional witness to the mystery of Christ' [*RM*, 27], has deepened its understanding of the mystery of the kenosis of the 'Son of God' (Lk 3:38; cf. Ph 2:5-8) who became in Mary 'Son of Adam' (Lk 3:38), and has recognized more clearly the historical roots of the 'Son of David' (cf. Lk 1:32), his place among the Hebrew people, his membership in the 'poor of Yahweh.'"[16]

Soteriology and Mariology

15. Through the meritorious death of Christ[17] the Blessed Virgin was "redeemed in a more sublime manner" than other men and women[18]; through Christ's death she is "the most excellent fruit of the redemption,"[19] the "icon and model of humanity redeemed by Christ"[20]; as mother of the Redeemer and his "generous associate," she cooperated in a unique way "in the work of the Savior."[21] Through the consent which she offered to the redemptive Incarnation of the Word, through her loving service to the person and to the mission of the Redeemer, through her offering of self and her association with the sacrifice of her Son, through her continuous intercession in heaven and her maternal presence in the life of the Church, she has cooperated

---

[15] Paul VI, *Discourse at the Close of the Third Session*, in *AAS* 56 (1964), 1015. Cf. n. 5.

[16] *VMISF*, 19.

[17] Cf. Pius IX, *Ineffabilis Deus* (8 December 1854), in particular the text of the definition, in *MOC*, 9. Cf. Collect, Solemnity of the Immaculate Conception of the Blessed Virgin Mary (8 December), *Roman Missal*.

[18] *LG*, 53.

[19] *SC*, 103.

[20] John Paul II, *Discourse for the Participants of the Third Session of the Pontifical Academy* (7 November 1998) in the Italian edition of *OR* (8 November 1998), 7.

[21] *LG*, 61.

and continues to cooperate, through the gracious plan of God, with Christ for the salvation of humanity.[22]

Pneumatology and Mariology

16. Mary, the All-holy, is the first creature completely formed by the Holy Spirit (*pneumatophorme*)[23]; she is the vessel of the Holy Spirit (*pneumatophora*), whose life was so animated and guided by the divine Spirit[24] that she is rightly considered the icon of the Spirit. According to the contemplative tradition of the Church, the Spirit brought forth from the heart of Mary her salvific fiat (cf. Lk 1:38) and her canticle of praise, the *Magnificat* (cf. Lk 1:46-55). The Spirit formed in the humble Mary an attitude of worship which changed the ritual of reclaiming her child at the Presentation in the Temple (cf. Lk 2:22-24) into a prelude of offering him as the redeeming lamb.[25] The Spirit was the reason that the mother addressed her Son in favor of the guests at the wedding feast of Cana (cf. Jn 2:3) and for the exhortation she directed to the servants that they "do whatever he tells you" (Jn 2:5). The Spirit sustained the Virgin in her great sorrow at the foot of the cross and inflamed her heart so that she might welcome the final wish of her dying Son making her the mother of his disciples (cf. Jn 19:26). The Spirit was

---

[22] Cf. *Ibid.*, 53, 56, 57, 58, 61, 62, 63; cf. John Paul II, General Audience (9 April 1997): *The Virgin Mary, Cooperator in the Work of Redemption*, in *OR* (10 April 1997), 11; "Mary's Cooperation Is Totally Unique," in *Theotókos: Woman, Mother, Disciple: A Catechesis on Mary, Mother of God*, Boston: Pauline Books & Media, 185-187.

[23] *LG*, 56.

[24] Cf. *MC*, 26; cf. *The Holy Spirit and Mary, Letter to Cardinal Leon Josef Suenens* (13 May 1975), in *TPS* (1975), 19-20; *Insegnamenti di Paolo VI*, XIII (1975), 493.

[25] Cf. Ambrose Aupert, *Sermo in purificatione sanctae Mariae* 3, 7: *CCCM* 27B, 987, 991-992; Bernard of Clairvaux, *In purificatione sanctae Mariae* III, 2: *SBO* IV, 342-343; *Liturgia della Ore*, Presentation of the Lord (2 February). Lauds, the hymn *Adorna, Sion, thalamum*, is the work of Peter Abelard († 1142).

the source of her faith in the Resurrection of Christ and made her the *Orante* at the Cenacle (cf. Ac 1:12-14), an exceptional Witness of Christ's infancy.

Ecclesiology and Mariology

17. The Mother of the Savior was actively present in the events which formed the Church. She was present at Nazareth and Bethlehem: according to an authoritative tradition, the conception and birth of Christ from the virginal womb of Mary included not only the Head but also the members of the Mystical Body, as Pope Leo the Great († 461) affirmed with these insightful and profound words: "The birth of Christ is the origin of the Christian people, and the birthday of the Head is also the birthday of the body."[26] She was present at Cana where the disciples of Christ "began to believe in him" (Jn 2:11), thus forming a community of faith around the Teacher; at the foot of the cross where, from the open side of Christ "as he slept the sleep of death upon the cross, there came forth 'the wondrous sacrament of the whole Church'"[27]; and in the Cenacle where the community of Jesus' followers received the gift of the Holy Spirit and where the Church and its universal mission were manifested (cf. Ac 2:1-40). The relation between ecclesiology and mariology is also evident in the way that the Church regards the Virgin Mother — its "preeminent member,"[28] its "most beloved mother,"[29] its complete image, and its prophetic type and

---

[26] *Sermone 26, 6 (Sul Natale del Signore, 6)*, in *PL* 54, 213B; in Michael O'Carroll, C.S.Sp., *Theotokos: A Theological Encyclopedia of the Blessed Virgin Mary*, Wilmington, Delaware: Michael Glazier, Inc., 218.

[27] *SC*, 5.

[28] *LG*, 53.

[29] Cf. *Ibid.*, 53; cf. Paul VI, *Discourse at the Close of the Third Session* (cf. n. 5).

figure,[30] and its eschatological icon.[31] In its completed structure and physiognomy, the Church has, as noted theologians and even John Paul II have pointed out,[32] a "Marian dimension." The divine profile of the Church is already present in the countenance of Mary of Nazareth.

Theological Anthropology and Mariology

18. The divine plan for humanity, present in a wonderful manner in the sacred humanity of Christ, the new man, finds a sublime realization in Mary, the new woman. At the very beginning of her existence, Mary, by her Immaculate Conception, was filled with grace (cf. Lk 1:28); at the end of her life, by her glorious Assumption, she, in the totality of her being, was completely transfigured into Christ. She in a wonderful way represents the process of predestination, election, justification, and glorification in Christ (cf. Rm 8:29-30)[33] to which every man and woman is called (cf. Eph 3:1-14). The Virgin Mary is the creature in whom liberty is harmonized with obedience to God, the aspiration of the soul with the values of the body, divine grace with human initiative.

---

[30] *LG,* 65.

[31] *SC,* 103.

[32] Cf. John Paul II, *Address to the Roman Curia* (22 December 1987), in *AAS* 80 (1988), 1026-1029; Apostolic Letter *Mulieris Dignitatem* (*MD*), (15 August 1988), 27, n. 55. *Letter to Women for Beijing Conference* (29 June 1995), 9, in *OR* (12 July 1995); *Catechism of the Catholic Church* (*CCC*), 773.

[33] Significantly, the Roman liturgy uses Romans 8:29-30 for the *Lectio brevis* for the Evening Prayer I of the Solemnity of the Immaculate Conception (8 December) as well as for the Solemnity of the Assumption (15 August).

19. Holy Mary is invoked in the liturgy as the "hope of God's people."[34] "Just as the Mother of Jesus, glorified in body and soul in heaven, is the image and beginning of the Church to be perfected in the world to come, so too does she shine forth on earth, until the day of the Lord shall come (cf. 2 P 3, 10), as a sign of sure hope and solace to the people of God during their sojourn on earth."[35] Rightly then does the Church "joyfully contemplate in Mary, as a faultless image, that which she herself desires and hopes wholly to be."[36] The Virgin is the Christian fully completed. In her is time compressed: the past, present, and future illuminate each other. In Mary *the yesterday* of Israel and the Church become present through the liturgical remembrance; *the today* is characterized by the active presence of Mary as the pilgrim Church journeys toward its ultimate goal; and *the tomorrow* is an assured reality, the basis of faith and hope. In her, the Glorified One, fear of the future is conquered, the enigma of death is overcome, unmasked by the glory now radiant with the light of the Resurrected One... who is the destiny of every person.

Mariology: A Discipline of Reclaiming the Tradition and of Synthesis

20. These are a few examples of the bonds between mariology and the various theological disciplines. Others could be added, but these suffice to show that mariology is a discipline of re-

---

[34] *Collection of Masses of the Blessed Virgin Mary* (hereafter *CMBVM*), 37: "The Blessed Virgin Mary, Mother of Divine Hope," Entrance Antiphon (New York: Catholic Book Publishing Co., 1992).

[35] *LG*, 68; cf. *Roman Missal*, Votive Mass, "Mary, Virgin Mother of the Church," Preface.

[36] *SC*, 103.

8

claiming the tradition, a space for the meeting of theological disciplines, and a place for synthesis.

From these many references it now becomes clear how mariology is the *relational discipline par excellence,* one completely different from an "isolated discipline," as it has frequently but erroneously been described. In Mary all is relative to *God the Father* of whom she is the humble and faithful servant (cf. Lk 1: 38, 48) and also the beloved daughter (*LG* 53)[37]; everything is relative to *Christ* of whom she is the true mother, the generous associate, the faithful disciple; everything is relative to the *Spirit* who has given her a "new heart and a new spirit" (Ezk 36:26), and has overshadowed her in order that from her virginal womb might be born the Savior (cf. Lk 1:35), and dwells in her as in a most pure temple and sanctuary. Everything in the daughter of Zion is related to *ancient Israel,* her people, of whom she is the personification, the culmination, and its purest expression; to the Church she is the preeminent member and its eschatological model; "in Mary everything is related to the human person, in all times and all places. She has a universal and permanent value."[38] In the Mother of God, all finally is related to the *universe* of which she is its vertex and highest adornment.

21. But, in addition to the task of retrieving, mariology is a place for synthesizing; the entire history of salvation, from the predestination *ab aeterno* of the Incarnate Word[39] to the *parousia* of the Lord, from Genesis to the Book of Revelation,[40] the Mother of Jesus is in some way enclosed and presented. This is why some theologians refer to the figure of Mary and to its

---

[37] *LG,* 53; John Paul II, Apostolic Letter *On Preparation for the Jubilee of the Year 2000. Tertio Millennio Adveniente (TMA),* (10 November 1994), 54, in *AAS* 87 (1994), 5-41; in *Origins* 24 (1994), 401ff.

[38] *VMISF,* 25.

[39] Cf. *Ineffabilis Deus,* Preface.

[40] Cf. *MC,* 30.

reflection in theology as "the key of Christian mystery," as the "icon of the mystery," as the "microcosm of salvation," as the "revelation's model," as the "intersection of theology," the place where "the nexus of the mysteries," in their varied and close interrelationships, is strikingly evident. For that reason, Vatican II perceptively observed that Mary, "since her entry into salvation history, unites in herself and re-echoes the greatest teachings of the faith."[41]

22. Let us now draw some conclusions from what we have said. To say that the Virgin Mary is a peripheral element of the Christian mystery, a marginal note of faith and theology, appears to us to be an altogether unacceptable position. The salvific Incarnation of the Word of God in which Mary, according to the design of God, participated with her fiat, which changed our history, was not a peripheral matter; neither were the words of Christ on the cross to his mother and to the disciple marginal details; and Pentecost was not an unimportant event.

Moreover, it appears that the various theological treatises ought to devote appropriate space to the part which the Mother of the Lord has in the mystery which is being studied. For example, it appears inexplicable that treatises of ecclesiology are written which do not devote a few pages to Mary, to the one from which the Church has taken her "Marian profile," and in whose qualities as virgin-spouse-mother, the Church recognizes its exemplary model and eschatological icon.

Finally, one can see how provident are directives of the Holy See indicating that mariology should be included among the subjects studied in theology: "Considering the importance of the Virgin in the history of salvation and in the life of the people of God, and after the promptings of Vatican Council II

---

[41] *LG*, 65.

and of the popes, it would be unthinkable that the teaching of mariology be obscured today: it is necessary therefore that it be given its just place in seminaries and theological faculties."[42] This directive, however, has not been given sufficient attention. Sometimes it has been disregarded; in other cases it was carried out without much conviction.

Sources of Mariology

23. Mariology does not have its own sources: it relies upon the same sources as any other theological discipline. *Lumen Gentium* enumerated them, as it exhorted theologians and preachers to correctly describe the role and the privileges of the Virgin Mary "following the study of Sacred Scripture, the Fathers, the doctors and liturgy of the Church, and under the guidance of the Church's magisterium."[43] So it seems opportune for us to share with you some considerations on the way mariology uses its sources, beginning with that which is primary — the Word of God.

Sacred Scripture

24. With extraordinary lucidity, Vatican II teaches that "sacred theology rests on the written word of God, together with sacred tradition, as its primary and perpetual foundation. By scrutinizing in the light of faith all truth stored up in the mystery of Christ, theology is most powerfully strengthened and constantly rejuvenated by that word."[44] What is said here is entirely applicable to mariology.

---

[42] *VMISF,* 27.
[43] *LG,* 67.
[44] *Dei Verbum (DV),* 24; cf. *Optatam Totius (OT),* 16.

11

Here we note the great progress made by mariology in the twentieth century was due principally to a thorough and detailed study of biblical texts regarding the Mother of the Lord. This is not the place to list the catalog of these achievements, but to express to biblical scholars the gratitude of the Pontifical International Marian Academy and, we feel also certain, of all the mariological societies.

Concerning the use of Sacred Scripture in mariological research, a few considerations appear opportune:

— Exegetes now use a variety of approaches for dealing with the Bible.[45] Such variety is legitimate provided that, avoiding fundamentalism on the one hand, we do not neglect the literal sense of the Scriptures (to which the historical critical method has made a great contribution) and, on the other hand, we do not undervalue the special characteristic of the Bible as the inspired Word of God transmitted in human language by many holy scribes throughout the centuries, welcomed by the community of faith, which possesses theological certitude (the self-revelation of God) and a soteriological mission (the salvation of humanity). In this variety of approaches, the principle enunciated at Vatican II has lasting value: The Sacred Scripture "must be read and interpreted with its divine authorship in mind; no less attention must be devoted to the content and unity of the whole of Scripture, taking into account the Tradition of the entire Church and the analogy of faith."[46]

— In mariology the principle regarding "the unity of the whole of Scripture" has fruitful applications: As *one book,* it has *one* author, *one* people to whom it is addressed, and

---

[45] Cf. Pontifical Biblical Commission, *The Interpretation of the Bible in the Church* (21 September 1993); *Origins* 23 (6 January 1994), 497.

[46] *DV,* 12.

one destiny which it prefigures. This principle serves to unite, not in any arbitrary way, the woman of Genesis 3:15 with the woman of John 2:5 and 19:26 and, finally, with the woman of the Book of Revelation 12:1. Similarly, it invites us to see the continuity of the *blessing* women have received for the liberating mission of Israel: Jael (Jg 5:24), Judith (cf. Jdt 15:9-10), Mary of Nazareth (cf. Lk 1:42). The reference to the "living tradition of all the Church" should convince us not to bypass in our mariological studies the patristic exegetes. The Fathers are at the heart of the tradition and they are the indispensable teachers of an ecclesial-theological reading of the Bible carried out with an authentic Christian spirit which is of incomparable value.[47]

— It would be well not to repeat constantly, as a refrain, that the Scriptures say very little about Mary; in this regard John Paul II has pointed out that "...after the Apostle Peter and John the Precursor, the Blessed Virgin is the person most mentioned in the canonical Gospels."[48] In the Gospel texts dealing with the Virgin Mary what is important is the quality, not the quantity, of the passages: the story of the Annunciation (Lk 1:26-38), of the Visitation (Lk 1:39-56), of the wedding feast at Cana (Jn 2:1-12), of the mutual entrustment of the disciple to the mother and of the mother to the disciple (Jn 19:25-27) — these are among the most profound and significant passages of the Gospel.

---

[47] Cf. Congregation for Catholic Education, *Inspectis Dierum, Instruction on the Study of the Fathers of the Church in the Formation of Priests* (10 November 1988), 26-29, in *AAS* 82 (1990), 618-620; in *Origins* 19 (25 January 1990), 549f.

[48] John Paul II, *Address to the Pontifical Theological Faculty "Marianum,"* 4, in *AAS* 81 (1989), 774; in *OR* (16 January 1989), 6-7.

Sacred Tradition

25. According to Catholic doctrine, divine revelation, which in Jesus, "the Father's one, perfect and unsurpassable Word,"[49] attained its highest expression, is transmitted in two ways: *written and unwritten* (orally), by which the "deposit of faith" (cf. 1 Tm 6:20) is found both in Sacred Scripture and in Sacred Tradition.[50] Moreover the East and the West accept and venerate "both Sacred Tradition and Sacred Scripture... with the same sense of loyalty and reverence."[51] Both constitute "the one sacred deposit of the word of God, entrusted to the Church."[52]

Among those who have studied and transmitted the truths of Sacred Tradition are, above all, the holy Fathers. From the second and third century, with the assistance of the Holy Spirit, in matters relating Christology to mariology, and ecclesiology to mariology, they explained the rich content of Sacred Tradition — such as the antithetical parallelism between Eve and Mary and the profound relation between Mary and the Church. This assiduous study of the tradition did not stop in the patristic epoch. It progressed continuously in the Church because the Spirit wished to lead it to possess truth in its entirety (cf. Jn 16: 13) in matters related to the person and the role of the Mother of Jesus in the history of salvation.

Theologians cannot omit the study of Sacred Tradition. In this way they will render an ecclesial service if, with rigor and personal commitment, they carefully separate that which is the content of the apostolic tradition, and what is closely associated with it, from "the various theological, disciplinary, liturgical or

---

[49] *CCC*, 65; cf. *Ibid.*, 102.
[50] Council of Trent, Session IV, April 1546, Decree *De libris sacris et de traditionibus recipiendis*: *DS* 1501; in J. Neuner and J. Dupuis, *The Christian Faith*, 7th ed., 102. Vatican I Dogmatic Constitution *Dei Filius*, chap 2: *DS* 3006; in Neuner and Dupuis, 104; *DV*, 8; *CCC*, 76-78.
[51] *DV*, 9; cf. *DS* 1501.
[52] *DV*, 10.

devotional 'traditions,' born in the local churches over time."[53]

In this regard, a systematic study of the data of tradition regarding the Mother of the Savior is important even when the matters may not have been part of the inspired apostolic era. Such recovery will enlighten the origins and the developments of many Marian devotional practices, of many texts, and of later doctrinal developments. Awareness of that which was previously unknown can awaken a sense of wonder. It is an immense field of research which the faith-filled spirit can explore with advanced historical methods and, significantly, with recourse to the history of mariology.

The Liturgy

26. We agree that students of mariology should devote attention, more than they have in the past, to the liturgy, which is a most noble part of Sacred Tradition. The apostle Paul affirmed the truth of Christ's Resurrection and the meaning of the Eucharist by an identical formula: "For I handed on to you (the *tradition*) as I also received" (1 Cor 15:3; cf. 11:23).

The liturgy, which is composed of "immutable elements divinely instituted, and of elements subject to change,"[54] is rightfully recognized as an indispensable *locus theologicus,* that is, an expression of the faith and the doctrine of the Church — the justification for the adage *legem credendi lex statuat supplicandi.*[55] The liturgy truly manifests, in a decisive way, the faith of the Church.

The great value of the liturgy in determining the faith of the Church is derived from its celebration of the mystery of

---

[53] *CCC,* 83.

[54] *SC,* 21.

[55] *Indiculus de gratia Dei et libero voluntatis arbitrio* VIII: *DS* 246; cf. *Ineffabilis Deus* (in *Pii IX Pontificis Maximi Acta,* I, p. 601); *MC,* 56.

Christ and the entire history of salvation. From this point of view, the liturgy is the Church's "faith celebrated," and Christian antiquity, especially the East, regarded it as *fundamental and primary*, the highest expression of theology.

As the "faith celebrated," certain truths regarding the Mother of God, for example her heavenly intercession, long before they were the object of theological reflection or of doctrinal pronouncements, were clearly asserted in the liturgical celebration of the saving mystery.

27. To appreciate fully the value of the liturgy as a source of theological reflection we should be aware of the following:

— In harmony with the intimate nature of the liturgical celebration of the mystery of salvation, the liturgy, in the celebration of the liturgical year, points out *the participation of the mother in the redemptive work accomplished by her Son* to whom she is united by an indissoluble bond. This participation has a certain passive aspect, insofar as Mary was a creature redeemed, although in "a more exalted fashion,"[56] but it also has an active dimension in that, according to the divine plan, she was *the generous associate of the Redeemer.*[57]

— The liturgy points out the exemplary holiness of the Mother of God; the liturgy "with its wonderful power of bringing to mind the realities and events of the past and of making them present here and now... presents... the image of the Virgin of Nazareth... who shines radiantly as the 'exemplar of virtues'"[58]; this powerful example of Mary

---

[56] *LG,* 53.
[57] *LG,* 61.
[58] *CMBVM,* Introduction, "The Blessed Virgin Mary in the Celebration of the Mystery of Christ," 14.

"urges the faithful to become like the Mother, in order that they might be fashioned more completely in the likeness of her Son" and "to treasure the word of God in their hearts and dwell upon it assiduously; to praise God exultantly and thank him joyously; to serve God and neighbor faithfully and offer themselves generously; to pray with perseverance and make their petitions with confidence; to act in all things with mercy and humility; to cherish the law of God and embrace it with love; to love God in everything and above everything else; to be ready to meet Christ when he comes."[59]

— The liturgy accents *the presence of the Virgin Mary in the worshiping assembly.* She is the preeminent member of God's royal and priestly people; now fully glorified, Mary participates in the worship of the Church. In the *today of the liturgy,* the voices of the angels and of the saints and, above all, of the "ever-virgin mother of Jesus Christ our Lord and God"[60] are joined to those of Christ and the Church in their prayer and intercession, in offering the sacrifice and celebrating the Sacraments.[61] In the liturgical celebration, Mary, through her heavenly intercession and by her role in the Mystical Body, is *in* the Church and *with* the Church, and she is continuously involved in this activity as mother of the risen Christ and all the living.[62]

---

[59] *Ibid.,* 17.

[60] *Roman Missal,* Roman Canon, *Communicantes.*

[61] *SC,* 7.

[62] *Marialis Cultus* describes the relations between Mary and the liturgy when it presents the Virgin as "model of the spiritual attitude with which the Church celebrates and lives the divine mysteries. That the Blessed Virgin is an exemplar in this field derives from the fact that she is recognized as a most excellent exemplar of the Church in the order of faith, charity and perfect union with Christ, that is, of that interior disposition with which the Church, the beloved spouse, closely associated with her Lord, invokes Christ and through him worships the eternal Father" (16); cf. *CMBVM,* Introduction, 17.

— The liturgy is a *living, reliable, and comprehensive* source. It is *living* because the liturgy is not an encrusted collection; rather it is a living celebration, and only in such a celebration do the ceremonies and words reveal in a full and existential way their profound meaning; it is a *reliable* source, the fruit of a long process in which the experience of the worshiping community and the approbation by a competent authority together become instruments providing a sure guarantee; it is a *comprehensive* source because in the liturgy are the inexhaustible riches of the Scriptures and the tradition of the Fathers as found in the sapiential path traced in the history of salvation; it also includes the contributions of art and literature, both animated by faith and by the guidance of the Spirit (cf. Rm 8:26-27).

The Magisterium of the Church

28. In the development of mariology the Church's magisterium has had a considerable role, almost to the point that some believe it is mariology's principal source. But the magisterium is not properly speaking a source. Vatican II stated that the "teaching office is not above the word of God, but serves it,"[63] and that "sacred tradition, Sacred Scripture and the teaching authority of the Church, in accord with God's most wise design, are so linked and joined together that one cannot stand without the others."[64]

In mariology, the magisterium has always been vigilant, by recourse to the Scriptures, to curtail deviant doctrines regarding Mary's virginity and the divine motherhood; diligent in discerning the biblical foundation of the Church's devotion to the Mother of God; attentive to single out in a few biblical

---

[63] *DV,* 10.
[64] *Ibid.,* 10.

verses a *sensus plenior* concerning the person and the mission of the Virgin Mary; solicitous to bring together, from the whole biblical text, the revelation on important points of doctrine — the Immaculate Conception and the glorious Assumption. Because these doctrines ultimately deal with the truth found in Sacred Scripture,[65] the magisterium did not hesitate to proclaim them doctrines of faith.

Regarding the role of the magisterium in mariology, two attitudes are to be avoided:

— a *disregard* of its function, caused by a type of reaction to the preponderant role which in the past the magisterium had in mariology; such disregard deprives Marian research of a valid instrument of discernment and of a valuable guide for exploring the theological sources, beginning with Sacred Scripture itself;

— the *improper use* of the magisterium which, in some circumstances, included various "testimonies" including many addresses of bishops and even of popes, for example, their greetings to groups of the faithful, occasional writings, commemorative discourses, ceremonial addresses, and minor allocutions — which were not intended to be expressions of the authentic magisterium.

Appeals to the magisterium of the Church should be made in an accurate way and with much precision. The contextual elements in which the statements are found should be the object of a very careful study.[66] Only under these conditions will recourse to the magisterium be respected and serve as a guide for research.

---

[65] Both Pius IX and Pius XII recognized that the ultimate foundation for the dogmas of the Immaculate Conception of the Virgin Mary and of the Assumption of her body and soul into heaven was Sacred Scripture. Cf. *Ineffabilis* in *MOC*, 17f.; *Munificentissimus*, in *AAS* 42 (1950), 767-768, 769. *MOC*, 38f.

[66] *LG*, 25.

29. The *sensus fidelium* has had an important role in the development of Marian doctrine, in particular in the path leading to the definition of the dogmas of the Immaculate Conception and of the Assumption. This is true, but the statement requires much precision, so that it may not be misunderstood. Some assert that it is a sign of the weakness of Marian doctrines which, because they do not have a solid biblical foundation, must rely on the pious sentiments of the faithful. With language taken from the political sphere, they add that the *sensus fidelium* is a type of political pressure to which the magisterium has often succumbed to accommodate the sentiments of the pious and devout. Such an idea of the *sensus fidelium* is unacceptable both from a doctrinal and a historical viewpoint.

Here the following should be kept in mind:

— The *sensus fidelium* cannot be separated from the *sensus Ecclesiae,* made up of "consensus of the bishops and of the faithful,"[67] found in the sacred liturgy, in ecclesial structures, and in many other expressions of the Church's tradition.

— The *sensus fidelium* cannot be thought of as a reality separate from the magisterium, but as a reality in close contact with the teaching of the bishops, for which it provides the reflection and the foundation in the body of the Church. Throughout the centuries the *sensus fidelium* has been part of the doctrinal developments on the Virgin Mary, discerning with great insight which specific proposals were most conformable to the wise plan of God. The faithful understood the reasons of the bishops assembled for the Council of Ephesus (431) who maintained the legitimacy of the title *Theotokos* conferred on the one who had con-

---

[67] *Ineffabilis,* in *Pii IX Pontificis Maximi Acta,* I, 598, 615. *MOC,* 16f.

ceived and given birth to the Divine Word in his human nature. They also understood that it was consonant with the ineffable mystery of the divine and virginal maternity of the one who became the holy temple of God, the holy land, the burning bush, the "eastern gate" open to the Lord alone (cf. Ezk 44:11),[68] who was to remain the "ever-virgin" and "virgin forever," with no other children. The faithful understood that the very holiness of God required that the creature predestined to be the beloved daughter of the Trinity (cf. Is 6:3; Rv 4:8), the mother of God's Holy One (cf. Mk 1:24; Ac 3:14), and the dwelling place of the Spirit, was never subject, not even for the briefest moment, to the dominion of Satan, and that from the first moment of her conception she was adorned with the grace of the Spirit. Similarly, in matters related to the Assumption of Mary, Pius XII wrote, "Christ's faithful, through the teaching and the leadership of their pastors... did not find it difficult to admit that the great Mother of God, like her only begotten Son, had actually passed from this life. But this in no way prevented them from believing and from professing openly that her sacred body had never been subject to the corruption of the tomb, and that the august tabernacle of the Divine Word had never been reduced to dust and ashes."[69]

These are some of the contributions which the *sensus fidelium* has made to mariology and which the magisterium has warmly welcomed. Fundamental to the *sensus fidelium* is the fact that the faithful participate in the prophetic function of Christ[70] and have received the Spirit of truth "who scrutinizes

---

[68] Proclus of Constantinople, *Oratio VI. Laudatio sanctae Dei Genitricis Mariae*, XVII: *PG* 65, 756A.

[69] *Munificentissimus*, in *AAS* 42 (1950), 757-758.

[70] *LG*, 12.

21

everything, even the depths of God" (1 Cor 2:10). The faithful frequently are those "little ones" to whom the Father has revealed the mysteries of the kingdom (cf. Mt 11:25-26).[71]

After a time when theological research overlooked the *sensus fidelium*, Vatican II pointed out that the laity — men and women — are active subjects both in the understanding of the deposit of revelation[72] and of the process of its transmission: "Christ, the great Prophet... continually fulfills his prophetic office until the complete manifestation of glory. He does this not only through the hierarchy who teach in his name and with his authority, but also through the laity whom he made his witnesses and to whom he gave understanding of the faith (*sensus fidei*) and an attractiveness in speech."[73]

The directives of the council should be welcomed in contemporary mariological reflection. Students of mariology should value the *sensus fidelium* and, for example, make use of the specific contribution that women can make to a deeper understanding of Mary of Nazareth, the woman *par excellence.*

Theological Method

30. In the post-conciliar era theological research was characterized by a plurality of methods which served as an approach to understanding the deposit of faith, for reflection on the principal doctrines of faith, and for organizing these doctrines in well-defined lines in a coherent, organic way. This plurality of methods, influenced by the orientations and the perspectives

---

[71] John Paul II, *Mother of the Redeemer. Redemptoris Mater (RM)*, 17, in *AAS* 79 (1987): 361-433; in *MOC*, 247ff.

[72] *DV,* 8.

[73] *LG,* 35.

of chapter 8 of *Lumen Gentium*, was evident in the doctrinal reflection on the Blessed Virgin. While not suggesting that one method is preferable to another, allow us to make the following six observations.

Reference to Salvation History

31. It appears best to maintain, whatever theological method is chosen, a constant reference to the history of salvation[74]; this involves *a constant recourse to the holy Scripture* which, in its totality, narrates the patient condescension of God our Savior toward humanity. This approach characterized the *theology of the Fathers* who first discerned distinct ages and characters within salvation history. This approach is mindful of the *ceaseless flow of time* in which the history of the world and of the Church appear as *moments* of salvation history; it is characteristic of the *liturgy*, which in its celebration of salvation history, celebrates its fundamental event: Christ, the alpha and omega of all history (cf. Rv 1:8); Christ awaited, born in the fullness of time (cf. Gal 4:4), who, after his death and Resurrection, is glorified at the right hand of the Father, and is present to his Church until the end of the world (cf. Mt 28:20). He is constantly invoked (cf. Rv 22:17) as the Church awaits his second coming in glory. Now, through the indissoluble bond which unites the mother to the Son, Mary participates, although in a subordinate way, in the various stages of salvation history.

---

[74] In addition to dogmatic theology, Vatican II stated, "Let the other theological disciplines be renewed through a more living contact with the mystery of Christ and the history of salvation," *OT,* 16.

32. From these considerations flows the desire to enlarge mariology's frame of reference and context. In the wise synthesis of Vatican II the context is one of Christ and of the Church: "The Blessed Virgin Mary, Mother of God, in the Mystery of Christ and the Church."[75] Now this context can be considered in its vertical and horizontal dimensions: vertically Mary is viewed in a Trinitarian perspective because of the threefold relation — necessary and constitutive — which she has with the three Divine Persons[76]; horizontally, Mary is viewed in her relation, first to the Church, and then to humanity and the universe. Here there is a vast network of relationships, an immense context embracing many peoples with their own history and culture.

The "Way of Beauty"

33. In 1975, Paul VI pointed out to students of mariology that "to present Mary in an adequate way to the people of God," there exists alongside of the way of truth, that is of "biblical, historical, and theological speculation" — the work of scholars — a path "accessible to all, including the least educated: It is the path of beauty.… In fact, Mary is the creature 'all beautiful': she is the mirror without spot, and the supreme ideal of perfection which the artists of every period have endeavored to reproduce in their works. She is the 'woman clothed with the sun' (Rv 12: 1), in whom the purest rays of human beauty mingle with those

---

[75] Title of chapter 8 of the Dogmatic Constitution *Lumen Gentium*.

[76] John Paul II, General Audience of 10 January 1996: "Mary's Relationship with the Trinity," in *Insegnamenti di Giovanni Paolo II*, XIX/1 (1998), 46-49; *Theotókos: Woman, Mother, Disciple* (Boston: Pauline Books & Media, 2000), 57-60.

sovereign inaccessible rays of supernatural beauty."[77]

This observation of Paul VI took many theologians by surprise because of its novelty. Still, the *way of beauty*, transcending the category of a simple pastoral instrument, has become, although with a certain reluctance and with some questions, "an instrument of theological investigation." This development has been helped by the increasing attention given to theological aesthetics. Theologians are becoming aware of the aesthetical dimension of many pages of Sacred Scripture, and they are influenced by many literary works of the Fathers in which there occur striking expressions of the desire for beauty. Such expressions are found in the symbolic world of the liturgy and in the magnificent theological synthesis of the Middle Ages, which attempted to harmonize logic with a profound sense of mystery. Many contemporary theologians reflect these mystical orientations in their works.

The *tota pulchra* is in most intimate union with God, the very source of all beauty, and she copiously reflects the source from which she was formed: transfigured into a hymn of praise and gratitude, Mary — after Christ — pours out on the world beauty and sends it back to the source from which it came.

The hesitations of some theologians to embark upon this *way of beauty* are understandable: it uses the language of symbolism and provides poetic intuition and artistic inspiration as material for theological elaboration. But, it should be noted that the roots of symbolic language are found in creation and in history, and that the beauty which is the result of artistic activity has, as John Paul II stated in his *Letter to Artists* (4 April 1999), "transcendent value and its aura of mystery."[78] Our opinion is that the way of beauty, so congenial to the figure *tota pulchra*,

---

[77] "Message to the Participants at the 7th International Mariological Conference and the 14th Marian Conference at the Antonianum" (Rome, 16 May 1975), in *AAS* 67 (1975), 338; in *OR* (5 June 1975), 3-4.

[78] John Paul II, *Letter to Artists* (4 April 1999), no. 12, in *OR* (28 April 1999)

should not be neglected. The theological value of Marian iconography should be studied not only from a formal and artistic viewpoint, but also, as a component of liturgical celebration, it is an expression of Marian doctrine and devotion.

The "Way of Experience"

34. The lives of the saints are "the living exegesis" of the meaning of the Gospel. Under the guidance of the Spirit they have admirably put into practice the admonition of Jesus, "I have given you a model to follow, so that as I have done for you, you should also do" (Jn 13:15), and sensing superbly the sentiments of the Master, they have interpreted his teaching in a vivid manner. In our time, many theologians propose that theological consideration should be given to the experience of the holy ones or, as others prefer to say, to the "theology of the saints." After avoiding for a long time "experience" as a part of theological research, Vatican II did not hesitate to affirm that the understanding of Scripture "happens through the contemplation and study made by believers… through a penetrating understanding of the spiritual realities which they experience."[79] In today's fast-moving culture, theology does not attempt so much to be an "investigation of truth" as to be "a reflection on experience." It should be noted that "the way of experience" puts forth a knowledge from divine revelation acquired, not through speculation, but through a personal encounter of believers with that which they have welcomed in a deeply personal way into their lives. "I know him in whom I have believed" (2 Tm 1:12), as St. Paul exclaimed referring to his meeting with the Risen Lord on the Damascus road.

The "theology of the saints" has a sapiential character, the

---

[79] *DV,* 8.

26

result of a loving familiarity with the Scriptures; it is a theology which, while deeply rooted in tradition, is often innovative, not through producing immediate results, but rather through something which perdures. Its certification is its presentation of Christian life, which has been adopted with great profit by many of the faithful.

Among the many questions raised about the value of the "theology of the saints," no doubt, one — through its affirmation that Christianity is not in the first instance doctrine, but an encounter of life, the divine life which flows from the Father through Christ in the Spirit — has contributed to overcome the division between academic theology and the Christian life. The "theology of the saints" is truly a valuable and authoritative part of the Church's Tradition.

35. In mariology the saints have made an outstanding contribution to Marian doctrine and to the development of devotion to the Mother of the Lord. In these "encounters" of the saints with Mary, there are many insights illuminating the revealed texts on Mary and the attitudes necessary for interpreting them. For the saints, the Virgin Mary has become a significant figure in following Christ.

Thus, to provide a few examples, Saint Athanasius († 375) and Saint Ambrose († 397) perceived that the Mother of Jesus played an exemplary role (*norma vivendi, exemplar virtutum...*) and has instructive value in the Church (*magistra*), especially in matters related to consecrated virgins. Saint Ildephonsus of Toledo († 667), as he proclaimed himself the servant of Jesus, God and the Lord of glory, came to understand that he also should be the servant of the Lord's Mother. This attitude of service has been characteristic of other saints such as Odilo of Cluny († 1049) and Saint Peter Damien († 1072); this custom, with profit to many, continues down to the present.

Saint John Damascene († 749) had the experience of living

in constant union with the Mother of God — "On her, I medi-tate day and night"[80]; he strongly affirmed Mary's presence in the midst of the ecclesial community. Also in the East, six centuries later, the writings of Gregory Palamas, monk of Mount Athos and later archbishop of Thessalonika († 1359), are imbued with his lived experience. From his "experience of God" flowed also his "experience of Mary," which he described in several famous homilies given on Marian feasts.

Saints Anselm of Canterbury († 1109) and Bernard of Clairvaux († 1153), both mystics and theologians and recog-nized as "Marian doctors," had an experience of Mary's presence. Anselm joined a reverent homage of the sinner to the Queen of Mercy with the consciousness of being her child: "The Mother of God is our mother."[81] Bernard joined a confident abandonment to Mary with a constant call for her intercession. Saint Francis of Assisi (1226), mystic and poet, was profoundly grateful to Mary because, through her, Jesus became our brother, and he experientially sensed the profound unity between Mary and the Church and the bond of unity between the Virgin of Nazareth and the Holy Spirit. In the preaching of Saint Bernardine of Siena († 1444), learned and austere friend of humanists and also a popular preacher, were found Marian themes, and they represent a pinnacle of his theological vision — fruit of study, of a loving meditation on the word of God, and of a deep expe-rience of the saving mystery.

In the Middle Ages, there were also saints, mystics, and theologians who, through their pondering of the Scriptures and their contemplation of the Word Incarnate, arrived at a strik-ingly personal acquaintance with the Mother of God. Among

---

[80] *Homilia III*, in *Dormitione beatae Mariae Virginis* 1: *PG* 96, 753C; in *Theotókos,* 199.

[81] *Oratio VII.* "Ad sanctam Mariam pro impetrando eius et Christi amore," in M. Corbin & H. Rochais, *L'Oeuvre d'Anselme de Cantorbéry* 5, 294, 1:127; 7. "Prayer to St Mary to ask for her and Christ's love," in *The Prayers and Meditations of St. Anselm with the Proslogion,* trans. Sister Benedicta Ward, S.L.G., New York: Penguin Books, 1973.

these were Hildegard of Bingen († 1179), Gertrude of Helfta († 1302), Angela of Foligno († 1309), Bridget of Sweden († 1373), Catherine of Siena († 1380). At the end of the seventeenth and the beginning of the eighteenth centuries, the figure of Saint Louis Marie Grignion de Montfort († 1716) appeared, who was able to express, in a striking and sapiential way, the meaning of and a method for devotion to the Mother of God. He proposed "consecration to Christ through the hands of Mary, as an effective means for Christians to live faithfully their baptismal commitments."[82] In the Enlightenment, the time in which the deductive method prevailed in theology, Saint Alphonsus Maria de Liguori († 1787) reacted by proposing a knowledge of the Blessed Virgin derived from the contemplation of the "great works" (cf. Lk 1:49) which God had accomplished in Mary (her *true glories*), and he valued popular devotion in which the faithful, full of confidence, turned to Mary in their need. Saint Thérèse of the Child Jesus († 1897), a woman of great intelligence and penetrating intuition, felt the deep need for presenting the figure of Mary, whom she loved dearly, in Gospel terms, which avoided excessive ornamentation — an approach which has much value today. Finally, the martyr of Auschwitz, Saint Maximilian Maria Kolbe († 1941), understood the entire person and mission of Mary under the sign of the Immaculata and stressed the importance of the Holy Spirit when speaking about Mary.

The "theology of the saints" presents an enormous patrimony for the student of mariology. It should not be bypassed, and, with respect for its distinctive characteristics, it should be integrated into the Church's field of Tradition to establish carefully its value and its appropriate use.

---

[82] *RM*, 48.

36. The task of the student of mariology today is complex. Precisely because mariology is a theological discipline characterized by convergence and relationships, it should be studied from an interdisciplinary perspective,[83] that is, with a continual reference not only to the other theological disciplines, but also to the human sciences, especially history, anthropology, psychology, and sociology.[84] Such requirements place the theologian in a difficult position: How can data coming from diverse sciences — first from the biblical revelation with the varied interpretations given throughout the centuries, with the diverse formulations of the ecclesial traditions, with the varied theological disciplines — be synthesized in an organic manner with the secular sciences, which have methods of research much different from theological disciplines?

The student of mariology needs much patience and humility, that is, an awareness that the challenge is to present an integrated mariological perspective, in which all details contributing to a grand design are still only a partial picture — frequently illuminating — of the theological panorama which here will never be completed. Nevertheless, the interdisciplinary perspective should not be bypassed, lest mariology again become an isolated theological discipline.

---

[83] *VMISF,* 29.
[84] *MC,* 34.

37. With a few noteworthy exceptions, the use of narrative theology in mariology appears very limited. It would be hasty to conclude that this method is not suitable for theological research. Some may consider this method lacking a well-defined physiognomy, with many questions left unanswered. On the contrary, this approach can lay claim to be *fundamental*: many pages of the New and the Old Testament are dedicated to 'narrating' the salvific interventions in our history; this approach can also employ the method of development used in analysis of the Scriptural narratives. It should also claim language as an instrument for the narratives which are a constitutive element of theological wisdom whose aim is to awaken the tradition which the account has for the ecclesial community. Moreover, the narrative, insofar as it is an experience of an encounter, looks not only to that which has happened in the past, but also to that which is happening today, that is, the action of God, of Christ, of the Spirit, of Mary in us. Such may appear to give priority to "the experience of Mary" over "reasoning about Mary." In other words, it points out the strength of narrative theology over argumentative theology.

Some students of mariology may regard the method of narrative theology far removed from classical theology which is expected to provide proof for its argument. They may consider the narrative as lacking the power to convince — that it is a method derived from the ineffectual approaches that were characteristic of the last decades of the twentieth century. Certainly the method of narrative theology should be better defined, but it does not lack value and advantages. Among them, it brings together the ample narrative material concerning Mary which is found throughout the centuries in the ecclesial tradition — from the apocrypha to the miracle accounts, from the Marian legends to the whole range of experiences of God's people who see Mary as a living person maternally interceding with Christ her Son.

We do not wish to indicate a preference for any method. Our only concern is that no way is excluded which leads to a deeper knowledge of the person and the mission of the Mother of the Lord, even if some of them, in their initial stages, may not be clear and precise.

PieroDani 001

II

THE THEMES AND CURRENT QUESTIONS RELATED TO THE MYSTERY OF THE MOTHER OF THE LORD

Some Tasks for Contemporary Mariology

38. As Mary of Nazareth was the servant of the Lord and her entire life was at the service of the redemptive work of her Son and of the infant Church, so mariology is a theological discipline of service. Through insights gained from the person and mission of the Virgin Mary, it is able to make a contribution to the discussion of some problems which today face the Church and humanity.

Mirror of the Trinity

39. We are invited to broaden mariology's context to include a Trinitarian perspective (cf. no. 32). This requires a return to the very source of Christ and Mary — God the Father; it means contemplating, with a heart full of faith, that ineffable eternal instant in which God the Father, the source of all being, decided *ab aeterno* on the Incarnation of his Son; it means allowing oneself to return to the very beginning of creation, when the Father, moved by love, created through his Word the world (cf. Jn 1:3), with all its goodness and beauty (cf. Gn 1:3, 10, 12, 18, 21, 25), and oriented it toward the Son (cf. Col 1:16); it means reliving the moment when God created man and woman in his image and likeness (cf. Gn 1:26-27) and breathed into them his life-giving breath (cf. Gn 2:7); it means looking to the future, to the new Adam and the new Eve.

It was the Father who "chose Mary for a *unique mission* in the history of salvation: that of being the Mother of the long-awaited Savior."[85] She is the *beloved daughter*[86]: *daughter* in that through her birth she belongs to the Father, who in eternity is the source of the divine Son and who in time gives life through grace to innumerable men and women, among whom is Mary of Nazareth. She is *beloved,* in that God has mercifully looked upon her (cf. Lk 1:48) and uniquely blessed her with wondrous gifts of grace for the mission which she was to fulfill.

Created in the image and likeness of God (Gn 2:22), Mary is the *icon* of the Father's mercy and tenderness, of his justice and sanctity, of his infinite perfection. She is the chosen daughter of Sion,[87] the personification of the chosen people, virgin, and also the faithful *servant* of covenant (cf. Lk 1:38), ready to carry out the will of God; she is also the *spouse* loved by God with a constant love (cf. Ho 2:21-22). As the Lord of glory who sits on high, God the Father looks upon his lowly servant (cf. Sg 113:5-6; Is 66:2); as the divine *Spouse* his love is directed to the Virgin Mary who is his delight (cf. Is 62:4-5).

Through the Father's eternal generation of the Son and through Mary's divine maternity, a gift of grace given in the "fullness of time" (Gal 4:4), both the Father and the Virgin Mary — and those two alone — are able to turn to Jesus and say in all truth, "You are my Son" (cf. Lk 3:22; 2:49).[88]

40. In relation to the Incarnate Word, Mary is truly *mother,* having, in his human nature, conceived him, given him birth, nourished, raised, and educated him. Between the Incarnate Word — Jesus — and Mary there exists an indissoluble filial-maternal bond by which she recognizes in her Son her God and Lord. He honors and loves her as mother and thanks her for the gift of human life. Mary is not only "the most excellent

---

[85] *TMA,* 54.
[86] *LG,* 53.
[87] *Ibid.,* 55.
[88] Cf. Anselm of Canterbury, *Oratio VII,* 1: 96-97 [See n. 81].

fruit of the redemption"[89] but also the generous *associate*[90] in the work of redemption, the faithful *disciple* who hears the word of God and receives it as the seed of life in her heart (cf. Lk 2:19, 51), as well as an outstanding witness of the important events of Christ's life.

In the Word Incarnate and in Mary, in their inseparable relationship, the infinite distance between the Creator and the creature has been bridged; they are the holy space of the espousals of the divine nature and human nature, the place where the Trinity is manifest in the history of salvation for the first time, and where Mary, the leading representative of Israel and the first member of the Church, represents the new humanity ready to enter, in obedient love, into the dialog of the covenant.

41. Reference has already been made to the relation between the Spirit of holiness and Mary *the all-holy*, in the section dealing with the relation between pneumatology and mariology (cf. no. 16). Here we limit ourselves to pointing out that in the years following Vatican II many studies, requested by the magisterium,[91] were made on the relation between the Holy Spirit and the Virgin of Nazareth. Here we wish to present a brief synthesis of some aspects of that relationship.

---

[89] *SC,* 103.

[90] *LG,* 61.

[91] "It is our task," asserts Paul VI, "to exhort everyone, especially those in the pastoral ministry and also theologians, to meditate more deeply on the working of the Holy Spirit in the history of salvation, and to ensure that Christian spiritual writings give due prominence to his life-giving action. Such a study will bring out in particular the hidden relationship between the Spirit of God and the Virgin of Nazareth, and show the influence they exert on the Church" (*MC,* 27).

The Spirit of Holiness

The Immaculate Conception of the Virgin was a moment in salvation history of the greatest importance. In the first moment of her existence, the Spirit, who would one day bring forth blood and water from Christ's pierced heart (cf. Jn 19: 34), descended on her. The Spirit filled Mary with heavenly grace (cf. Lk 1:28), momentarily stopping the contagion of sin which stains every human being who comes into this world. As an iconographer, he imparted the traits of the new heart promised by the prophets (cf. Jr 31:31; 32, 40; Ezk 11:19; 36: 25-26). In the grace of the Immaculate Conception, the Holy Spirit formed Mary into a new creature,[92] his dwelling place.[93] The Spirit overshadowed Mary at the dawn of her existence. She would have no need of holy signs, of being born "of water and the Spirit" (cf. Jn 3:5): Her baptism was the presence of the Spirit within her, in the depths of her being.

The Life-giving Spirit

In the Apostles' Creed we profess that Christ was "conceived by the power of the Holy Spirit and born of the Virgin Mary."[94] The Holy Spirit's role in the Incarnation of the Word is found in the Scriptures, both in word (cf. Lk 1:35; Mt 1: 20-21) and symbol. "As the *cloud* covered the tent of meeting and the glory of the Lord filled the dwelling place" (Ex 30:34), so the Spirit overshadowed Mary of Nazareth as she conceived the Author of Life in her womb in a wonderful and ineffable manner.

---

[92] *LG*, 56.
[93] Cf. *Ibid.*, 53.
[94] *Symbolum Apostolicum* (*Traditio Apostolica,* Latin version): *DS*, 10.

The Spirit of Prophecy

The visit of Mary to the house of Zechariah is an event in salvation history in which the Spirit is the principal actor; it anticipated the wonderful event of Pentecost. The Virgin is full of the Spirit, who came upon her in the moment of her Immaculate Conception and the virginal conception of Christ. Mary meets Elizabeth: here were two sanctuaries of life, two maternities by grace. In that meeting Elizabeth was "filled with the Holy Spirit" (Lk 1:41). Under the influence of the Holy Spirit, she recognized the wondrous maternity of Mary and saw that the Child within the young mother was the Lord, as she exclaimed, "Most blessed are you among women, and blessed is the fruit of your womb. And how does this happen to me, that the mother of my Lord should come to me?" (Lk 1:42-43). Mary responded with her canticle, the *"Magnificat* of the ages."[95] In this canticle, prompted by the Spirit, come together the canticles of Miriam (cf. Ex 15:20-21), of Deborah (cf. Jg 5:2-31), of Judith (cf. Jdt 16:1-17), and of Hannah (cf. 1 S 2:1-10). It is sung daily by the Church, the Christ's bride, as the eternal expression of its thanksgiving and praise.

The Offering Spirit

The presentation of Jesus in the temple (cf. Lk 2:22-38) has a strong pneumatological dimension. Simeon, symbolically representing Israel faithful to the covenant, was a man of the Spirit: "The Spirit was upon him" (Lk 2:26). The Holy Spirit brought Simeon to the temple, revealed to him the messianic identity of the Child, and placed on his lips a hymn of blessing to God, a canticle of joy, because his expectations had been

---

[95] *RM,* 20.

fulfilled (cf. Lk 2:29-32). The Spirit mysteriously revealed to him that the Son would be "a sign that would be contradicted" (Lk 2:34), and that the heart of the mother would be pierced by a sword (cf. Lk 2:35). Mary is also found in the temple, in obedience to the law (cf. Lk 2:22), but, as Ambrose Autpert († 784) observed, she was there "by the impulse of the divine Spirit."[96] The Blessed Virgin, enlightened by the Spirit, understood that what she had done was more than the ordinary ritual[97]: she offered to the Lord not only a pair of turtle doves — the offering of the poor (cf. Lk 2:24) — but also her Son, the innocent Lamb who, taking upon himself the sin of humanity, would be sacrificed for the salvation of all people. The ritual which the Virgin carried out was a Christian liturgy. It transcended the Jewish ritual — with its stone temple, its levitical priesthood, and its sacrificial offerings. Mary offered the true Paschal Lamb "in Spirit and truth" (Jn 5:24).

The Spirit of Transforming Love

The wedding feast of Cana is another event of great pneumatological significance. "It was the Holy Spirit who urged the compassionate Mary to ask her Son for that miraculous change of water into wine at the wedding feast of Cana, which marked the beginning of Jesus' activity as a wonder-worker and led his disciples to believe in him (Jn 2:11)."[98]

In the history of exegesis the wine at the wedding feast of Cana has been variously interpreted. It was understood, for example, as a symbol of the Gospel of Christ: In the fullness of time, the water of the prophetic word was changed by the

---

[96] *In purificatione sanctae Mariae*, 7: CCCM 27B, 991.
[97] Cf. *MC*, 20.
[98] Paul VI: Letter to Cardinal Suenens (May 13, 1975), in *Insegnamenti di Paolo VI*, 12, 493.

power of the Holy Spirit into the Gospel of Christ, the highest and most definitive form of revelation.[99] It was understood as a figure of the Eucharist in which the Spirit changed the wine of our tables into the precious blood of the Lord.[100] It was seen as a symbol of the Spirit: As the wine from the Spirit in the espousals of ancient Israel was lacking, Jesus, the messianic spouse, provided "good wine" (Jn 2:10) in abundance for the espousals of the new Israel. The jars, filled with water, became vessels of the Spirit,[101] which moved the hearts of the disciples to faith in the Master (cf. Jn 2:11). The wedding at Cana is a representative example of the synergism between the Spirit's transforming love and the Virgin of Nazareth.

The Spirit of the Covenant

Jesus' *hour* did not come at Cana (cf. Jn 2:4): it was on Calvary, the hour of his passion and glorification (cf. Jn 12:23, 27-29), the hour of the Spirit (cf. Jn 19:30), the hour of the blood poured out as sign of the eternal covenant. The mother was present at the "espousals through blood" of the Son, as she was present at the wedding feast at Cana. Christian tradition has seen as a gift of the Spirit "the strength that sustained her acceptance of the will of God, and the vigor that upheld her in her suffering at the foot of the cross."[102]

Mary stood at the cross — the new woman become the true "mother of all the living" (Gn 3:20): It was the hour for giving birth, the hour of her spiritual maternity (cf. Jn 16:21). The fiat pronounced at Nazareth extended "without wavering"

---

[99] Cf. Augustine of Hippo, *In Iohannis Evangelium,* Tractatus IX, 2: *CCL* 36, 91.
[100] Gaudentius of Brescia, *Tractatus II,* 31-33: *CSEL* 68, 31-32.
[101] Cf. Gaudentius of Brescia, *Tractatus VIII,* 46-49; *Tractatus IX,* 44: *CSEL* 68, 73-74, 89.
[102] *MC,* 26.

to Calvary.[103] "It was the Holy Spirit who filled the Sorrowful Mother with immense love, widening and deepening her heart, as it were, so that she might accept as a last testament from the lips of her Son her maternal mission with regard to John, the beloved disciple (Jn 19:26)): a mission which, 'as the Church has always understood it,' prefigured her spiritual motherhood toward mankind as a whole."[104]

The Spirit of the Cenacle

As the "Mother of Jesus," Mary, together with the Eleven, some women, his followers, and other disciples (cf. Ac 1:13-14) — "there was a group of about one hundred and twenty persons in the one place" (Ac 1:15) — was present in the midst of this messianic community on which the Spirit descended on the day of Pentecost (cf. Ac 2:1-4). Meditating on this presence of the Mother of Jesus in the pentecostal Cenacle, Christian tradition has discerned her exemplary and ecclesial role. The Virgin of the Cenacle, as the *Orante,* was in the community fervently imploring the Father to send the Spirit, as Jesus had foretold (cf. Lk 24:49; Ac 1:4-5). She is the *Mother of the Church* because there, in the community of the disciples, was the beginning of her maternal mission received shortly before her Son died on the cross (cf. Jn 19:25-27). She is the *Mother of Unity,* who, at the center of a varied group of disciples, helps them to become one in prayer, in which all (Ac 4:32) participate in a "communal life" (Ac 2:42). She is that presence of peace which was and continues to be part of the Church's life throughout history.

---

[103] *LG,* 62.

[104] Paul VI: Letter to Cardinal Suenens (May 13, 1975), in *Insegnamenti di Paolo VI,* 12, 493.

42. Between the Trinity and the Virgin Mary there is a relationship rooted in the eternal design for the Incarnation of the Word. The Incarnation created the indissoluble bond between the Creator — the Trinitarian God — and the creature, Mary, the servant of Nazareth. Contemplating this relation, the heart of the theologian and of the contemplative is filled with wonder because the unbridgeable distance between God and humanity has been filled by the condescension of the Word, who, putting aside his divine nature and "taking the form of a slave" (Ph 2: 7), became consubstantial with his mother's human nature.

Christian tradition has expressed this relationship in formulaic metaphors, such as Mirror of the Trinity (*Speculum Trinitatis*) and Icon of the Trinity (*Icona Trinitatis*), which attempt to express the inexpressible. They attempt to describe the way in which Mary's pure and grace-filled heart reflected the relation of love and communion which unites the three divine Persons.[105] The felicitous expression of Adam of Saint Victor († ca. 1192), Banquet of the Trinity (*Triclinium Trinitatis*), expresses the spiritual indwelling of the Three Persons in Mary, making her the Cenacle or the banquet hall (*Triclinium*) where the Father, the Son, and the Holy Spirit repose in reciprocal love and delight.[106] The spacial metaphors describing the dwelling of the Trinity in Mary are many, frequently coming from images of sacred objects found in the Old Testament. Thus the Blessed Virgin is called

---

[105] Cf. John Paul II, *To Friends of the Focolare Movement, OR* (11 February 1988), 22 & 24; *Insegnamenti di Giovanni Paolo II*, XI/2 (1988), 1659.

[106] "Salve, mater Pietatis / et totius Trinitatis, / nobile Triclinium" (Adam of Saint Victor, *Quatorze proses du XIIème siècle à la louange de Marie*. Presentation, translation, and notes by Bernadette Jollès. Prose *Salve, Mater Salvatoris*, 11, Brepols, 1994, 216).

temple of the Trinity,[107] *tabernacle,*[108] *altar,*[109] *sanctuary,*[110] *city,*[111] *palace,*[112] *throne,*[113] *regal hall,*[114] and *nuptial chamber.*[115] Sometimes the metaphors wish to show that Mary is a precious work of the whole Trinity: the *jewel* (*Trinitatis gemma*)[116] and *beautiful flower* (*Trinitatis rosa*).[117]

There are also expressions of a personal nature. Associate of the Trinity (*Socia Trinitatis*)[118] and servant of the Trinity (*Ancilla Trinitatis*)[119] refer to the cooperation, willed by the Trinity, that the Virgin contributed to making our salvation possible. Spouse of the Trinity (*Sponsa Trinitatis*)[120] refers to the nuptial union into which Mary entered as she welcomed the Trinitarian love and offered herself to God. The *dispensary* of the Trinity (*Eleemosinaria Trinitatis*)[121] refers to the dispensation of grace,

---

[107] *De beata Maria Virgine* (Leselied, 14th c.), 6: *Meerssemann* I, 217.

[108] Cf. *Anthologion di tutto l'anno* [Rito bizantino], Ufficio dell'Orthros feriale. Theotokíon del giovedì. Rome, Lipa Edizioni, 1999, 105.

[109] Cf. Antonio di Lantsee († 1492), *Psalterium beatae Mariae Virginis,* 1: *Meerssemann* II, 146; *Centinomium cum glossa,* 1, 101: *Ibid.,* 177.

[110] Cf. *Pro pallio beatae Mariae* (Reimgebet, 15th c): *Meerssemann* I, 211.

[111] Cf. G. Savonarola, "Esposizione sopra l'orazione della Vergine" [Ave Maria], *Marian Library Studies* 10 (1978), 90, II, 16-17.

[112] *Ibid.*

[113] Cf. Proclus of Constantinople, *Oratio V. Laudatio in sanctam Virginem ac Dei Genitricem Mariam,* II: *PG* 65, 717C.

[114] Cf. Acrostic Alphabet *Ave, arca deitatis* (14th c.), 19: *Meerssemann* I, 210.

[115] Cf. John of Geometra (9th c.), *Sermo in sanctissimae Deiparae Annuntiationem XXXIX*: *PG* 106, 846.

[116] "Gemma totius Trinitatis": *Meerssemann* II, 19, n. 1.

[117] Cf. Columba de Vinchio († ca. 1300), *Antiphonae "ad magnificam et benedictam Dominam,"* 7: *Meerssemann* II, 131.

[118] Cf. *Litanie fiamminghe* (15th c.), 16: *Meerssemann* II, 248.

[119] Cf. *Salutatio ad beatam Virginem* (Gruss-Orationen, 14th c.) 1: *Meerssemann* II, 172.

[120] "When our *Father's jubilus* was saddened by Adam's fall, so that he had to become angry, the Eternal Wisdom of the almighty Godhead intercepted the anger together with me. The Father chose me for his bride — that he might have something to love; for his darling bride, the noble soul, was dead. The Son chose me to be his mother; and the Holy Spirit received me as his beloved. Then *I alone was the bride of the Holy Trinity* and mother of orphans, and I brought them before God's eyes so that they might not all sink down, though some did" (Mechthild of Magdeburg, *The Flowing Light of the Godhead,* trans., Frank Tobin, New York: Paulist, 1998, 50-51); in *TMPM,* IV, 361.

[121] Cf. *Litanie fiamminghe* (15th c.) 4: *Meerssemann* II, 248.

which God puts in the hands of Mary, in order that from her it may come to God's people.

These metaphors, which are not exhaustive nor of the same value, indicate the continuity of the reflection which developed and expressed the intense and profound relation of the Trinitarian God with the humble Virgin of Nazareth.

The Incarnation of the Word
"by the power of the Holy Spirit, from the Virgin Mary"

43. At times, the constitutive elements of the essential nucleus of the faith are presented to us. Here it is found in the article of the faith in which we profess that the Son of God became man "through the power of the Holy Spirit born of the Virgin Mary,"[122] that is, in the classical patristic expression recalled at Vatican II, she conceived "not knowing man."[123]

The doctrine of the virginal conception of Christ is found in the Gospel of Matthew (cf. Mt 1:16, 18-25) and Luke (cf. Lk 1:26-38); the Church placed it in the venerable creeds — the Apostles' Creed and that of Nicene-Constantinople (381); it was taught by Ignatius of Antioch, Aristides, Justin, and Irenaeus.[124] The Fathers unanimously affirmed the teaching explicitly, and it is wonderfully expressed in all of the liturgies of the East and the West.

For the Fathers this article of faith, "born by the power of the Spirit from the Virgin Mary," has a biological and historical dimension, and all human intervention is excluded; it cannot

---

[122] *Apostles' Creed*, Latin version: *DS* 10.

[123] *LG*, 63.

[124] Ignatius of Antioch, *Smirnesi* I, 1: *SCh* 10:154; *Ephesus* XVIII, 2: *SCh* 10:86; Aristides, *Apologia* 2, 6 in C. Vona (ed.), *L'Apologia di Aristide*. Rome, Lateranum, 1950:136; Justin, *Dialogo* 54, 2; 63, 2; 68, 4; 76, 1-2; 84, 1; *Apologia* 1, 32, 9; 1, 32, 11; 1, 32, 14; 1, 33, 6; 1, 46, 5; Ireneaus, *Adversus haereses* 3, 16, 2: *SCh* 34:280; 3, 21, 5: *SCh* 34:362.

be understood merely as a type of moral virginity nor as a way of saying that divine grace was on the one who would be born of Mary.

The Incarnation of the Word in Mary through the work of the Holy Spirit is a truth which belongs to the *deposit of the faith* and is proposed by the Church as divinely revealed. That is why mythical interpretations of the narrative of Matthew 1:18-25 and Luke 1:26-38, which imply that the conception of Jesus was the result of an ordinary matrimonial union, are incompatible with the faith.

We believe that such theologians and exegetes are not sufficiently aware that "the task of authentically interpreting the word of God, whether written or handed on, has been entrusted exclusively to the living teaching office of the Church,"[125] which — through the creeds of the faith, the unanimous consent of the Fathers, explicit conciliar statements, and the ordinary universal teaching of the bishops — all agree on the authentic meaning of Matthew 1:20 and Luke 1:35. The faith of the Church in the virginal conception of Christ has always been so secure and explicit that it was never thought that a formal definition was necessary.

This interpretation of the magisterium does not limit the research of theologians and exegetes on the Gospel text, but rather, directs it to the meaning intended by God. The progress of Christology, and consequently of mariology, does not occur by putting forth serpentine texts of the second and third centuries from pagan circles hostile to the Church and clearly heretical, but in exploring the *truth* which we know only through reve-lation and by illustrating its *significance* in God's plan and in relation to other truths of the faith and to contemporary culture. Here lies a rich and exciting venture.

---

[125] *DV,* 10; *Dei Filius,* 3: DS 3001.

44. Through the unique character of the virginal conception of Christ, true Son of God and true Son of Mary, the virginity of the servant of the Lord was seen by the holy Fathers as a complex reality referring totally to the transcendent mystery of Christ's divinity. Already from the fourth century, the holy Fathers in many clear statements affirmed that Mary brought forth the Son of God by a "virginal birth." Pope Saint Leo the Great († 461) in the well-known *Letter to Flavianus* affirmed that Mary "gave birth to Jesus, retaining her virginity as she also conceived him in virginity."[126] Similarly, with great authority, the Lateran Council, 649, asserted that Mary "in these last times, has conceived by the Holy Spirit, without human cooperation, and gave birth to God's Word, the one proceeding from God from all eternity, while remaining a virgin after giving birth."[127] Vatican II used an exemplary liturgical formula[128] which affirmed Mary's virginity: "the birth of Our Lord, who did not diminish His mother's virginal integrity but sanctified it."[129]

45. From antiquity, the Church maintained that the correct interpretation of the Gospel texts which speak of the brothers and sisters of Jesus (cf. Mt 12:46; 13:55; Mk 6:3) eliminated the possibility that they are the biological children of Mary.[130] For that reason the Church, under the guidance of the Holy Spirit, celebrated, in the great liturgies of the East and West, Mary as "ever virgin," who, sacred to the Word, had no human partner.

---

[126] *Epistola Papae Leonis ad Flavianum Episcopum Constantinopolitanum,* 2, in *Acta Conciliorum Oecumenicorum (ACO)*, 2, II, I, 25.

[127] Lateran Council, *Actio V,* can. 3, in *ACO,* 2a Ser. 1, 371.

[128] Cf. Prayer over the Gifts for Mary's Nativity (8 September) in J. Deshusses (ed.), *Le Sacramentaire Grégorien,* Fribourg (Switzerland), Editions Universitaires, 1971, 268. This formula is derived from the most ancient manuscripts.

[129] *LG,* 57.

[130] Cf. Epiphanius, *Adversus Haereses* III, 78:6, 7, 8, 15: PG 42:705-708, 707-710, 709-712, 723-724; Jerome, *Adversus Helvidium* 10:14-17, 19: PL 23, 202-203, 206-212, 213; *In Matthaeum* II, 12:46-49: *CCL* 77:100-101; Ambrose of Milan, *De Institutione Virginis* 6:43-45; Sermo 14/II:142-144; *Epistula LXXI*, De Bonoso Episcopo: *CSEL* 82:7 10.

The task for theology today is to uncover and to illustrate why God the Father wished that the "Word, the source of incorruptibility,"[131] become incarnate by the power of the Holy Spirit and be truly born, but in a virginal way by a virginal mother. This is why theology should approach the mystery of Mary's virginity "with a heart full of faith and adoring respect"[132]; and it should, by examining the whole of Scripture,[133] point out the relation of Mary's unique virginity to the whole of revelation, and, in particular, to the mystery of the Church, who, as spouse of the Incarnate Word, is also virgin and mother: "By her preaching she brings forth to a new and immortal life the sons who are born to her in baptism, conceived of the Holy Spirit and born of God."[134]

The Gift and Sign of Mary's Immaculate Conception

46. On 8 December 1854, Blessed Pope Pius IX defined the Immaculate Conception in these terms: "We declare, pronounce, and define that the doctrine which holds that the most Blessed Virgin Mary, in the first instance of her conception, by a singular grace and privilege granted by Almighty God, in view of the merits of Jesus Christ, the Savior of the human race, was preserved free from all stain of original sin, is a doctrine revealed by God and therefore to be believed firmly and constantly by all the faithful."[135]

This definition was the result of a long historical process

---

[131] Irenaeus, *Adversus Haereses* III, 19:1: *SCh* 34:330.

[132] John Paul II, Address to the participants of the convention in commemoration of the sixteenth centenary of the Council of Capua (391-92): *Studying Mary We Learn Who Jesus Is* (24 May 1992), in *OR* (27 May 1992), 13, 4, in *AAS* 85 (1193), 664.

[133] Cf. *Ibid.,* 9.

[134] *LG,* 64.

[135] *Ineffabilis,* in *Pii IX Pontificis Maximi Acta,* I, p. 616; *DS* 2803.

which involved in different ways all of the Catholic Church: the faithful with their charism of *sensus fidei,* theologians with their careful doctrinal treatises, the popes with their responsibility of overseeing, moderating, clarifying, and defining. The dogma defined on 8 December 1854 was binding and irreformable. But, as with every dogmatic definition, it was stated in a precise cultural context and language, and influenced by its history. At the opening of Vatican II, John XXIII observed, "For this deposit of faith, or truths which are contained in our time-honored teaching, is one thing; the manner in which these truths are set forth (with their meaning preserved intact) is something else."[136] Nothing prevents, then, while preserving the original meaning of the doctrine, that it be further developed and expressed in terms which are comprehensible to different cultures. As regards the Immaculate Conception of the Virgin Mary, the observation of the International Theological Commission is apropos: "A later time cannot reverse that which was formulated in dogma under the assistance of the Holy Spirit as a key for the reading of the Scriptures. This does not exclude that new points of view may arise in the course of time and that new formulations may be sought."[137]

47. Contemporary theological reflection on the dogma of the Immaculate Conception of Mary should attempt to develop these "new points of view." For example, the dogma can be viewed in the *light of the salvific love of the Trinity.* Mary's Immaculate Conception was by *grace alone,* a totally gratuitous gift of God the Father, the Son, and the Spirit: it manifests that Mary was justified by grace alone, not by her own merits.

---

[136] John XXIII, *Gaudet Mater Ecclesia, AAS* 54(1962), 792; "The Council — At the Threshold of a New Era," Address at the Opening of the Council (11 October 1962), in *TPS* 8/3, 212-213.

[137] Pontifical Theological Commission, *Interpretation of Dogma* (October 1989), in *Origins* 20/1 (May 17, 1990), 10 (section C.I. 1.).

The doctrine of Mary's freedom from sin can be viewed in a *christological, soteriological,* and *paschal* dimension, that is, as a truth derived from the divinity of Christ and from the mission of the redeeming Lamb, whose salvation is accorded as a privilege to one creature — Mary of Nazareth — by which she is distinguished from every other creature.

Further Suggestions

— *Christological.* The doctrine is based on the impossibility — as the *sensus fidelium* rightly intuited — that the Word of God — totally and radically holy — could take human nature from a creature who, even for the briefest moment, was dominated by the evil one.[138] From this viewpoint, Mary's Immaculate Conception was a preliminary requirement for the Incarnation of the Word: the preparation of his "worthy dwelling place."[139]

— *Soteriological.* This doctrine shows the universality of redemption of which Mary is "the most excellent fruit,"[140] herself redeemed "by a sublime grace."[141] That Mary is holy

---

[138] *Ineffabilis* in *MOC;* Pius XII, *Fulgens Corona* (8 September 1953), in *AAS* 45 (1953), 581, in *MOC.*

[139] The need for a "worthy dwelling place" (*Dignum habitaculum*), for a "worthy mother" (*Digna Genetrix*) for the Divine Word, who would become incarnate, is found in liturgical texts which give the reason for the Immaculate Conception of Mary; see, for example, *Roman Missal,* the Solemnity of the Immaculate Conception of the Blessed Virgin Mary, 8 December, Collect and Preface. From this perspective, the Immaculate Conception is not so much a gift to the Virgin of Nazareth as a christological, even trinitarian, necessity: On the part of the Father, who prepared a radically and absolutely holy dwelling for the Son who eternally proceeds from him and is infinitely loved, it was also required by Divine Wisdom, which, in the liturgical context, "has built herself a house" (Pr 9:1), excluding any association with sin which would be absolutely incompatible with its holiness; and it was required by the Holy Spirit, the divine iconographer, who embellished with outstanding gifts of grace and of holiness the dwelling place for the Son from whom he eternally proceeds.

[140] *SC,* 103.

[141] *LG,* 53.

and immaculate in her love in the sight of God (cf. Eph 1: 4) is due to the redeeming blood shed by her Son (cf. Eph 1:7).[142]

Mary's Immaculate Conception invites us to view redemption as more than a deliverance from sin; it is a divine gift, an abundant outpouring of grace, which establishes the person of Mary in the dominion of love.

— *Paschal Mystery.* The expression "in view of the merits of Jesus Christ," taken from the definition of the doctrine, places the Immaculate Conception within the Paschal mystery, that is, in the blessed passion and glorious Resurrection of the Lord. Mary's Immaculate Conception is an anticipation and the first fruit of the Paschal mystery.

— *Pneumatological.* The Immaculate Conception can also be seen in a pneumatological dimension centered on the sanctifying presence of the Spirit in Mary's Immaculate Conception. In this way, the narrow term "preservation from original sin," which was part of the historical theological development culminating in the dogmatic definition of 1854, is enlarged with a positive element — the fullness of grace, the gift of the Spirit — a dimension which resounds in Eastern theology.

— *Ecclesiological.* The doctrine can also be seen in an ecclesiological dimension. Among the great works of the Lord, the Church recognizes the Immaculate Conception as the highest expression of God's design for his people, expressed in the bridal relationship. Mary is the prototype and, with great insight, the liturgy for December 8 places on the

---

[142] Evening Prayer (I & II) of the Common of the Blessed Virgin contains the New Testament canticle, Ephesians 1:3-10, affirming that "we have redemption by his blood" (v. 7). The precious blood of Christ (cf. 1 P 1:19) was Mary's salvation: The redemption which she received, "preservation from original sin" (Immaculate Conception of Mary), is part of the universal redemption accomplished by Christ.

lips of Mary the canticle of the city-spouse: "I exult for joy in the Lord… for he has clothed me in the garment of salvation and robed me in the cloak of justice, like a bride adorned with her jewels."[143] God is glorified because in the Immaculate Conception of the Virgin there is the "sign of favor to the Church at its beginning, and the promise of its perfection as the bride of Christ, radiant in beauty."[144] The Church sees Mary in Ephesians 5:25-27, the marvelous account of Christ's love for his spouse, the Church. "Christ loved the church. He gave himself up for her to make her holy, to present to himself a glorious church, holy and immaculate, without stain or wrinkle or anything of that sort."[145] The spousal and filial character of God's people, of which Mary is the personification and the perfect image, includes not only the ecclesial community as such, but also each of its members; the reading (Eph 1:3-6, 11-12) for the Mass for 8 December, recalls that the Father "has blessed us in Christ with every spiritual blessing in the heavens, as he chose us in him, before the foundation of the world, to be holy and without blemish before him" (cf. Eph 1:3-5). Viewed in this way, baptism, the immersion into the Paschal Mystery of Christ (cf. Rm 6:3-5), corresponds sacramentally to Mary's Immaculate Conception. At the baptismal font the newly baptized, il-luminated by the light of Christ, become adopted children of the Father — branches grafted into the vine, members of Christ's mystical body. They are enriched by the gifts of the Holy Spirit who makes them his dwelling place and clothes them in nuptial garments.

---

[143] *Roman Missal,* Solemnity of the Immaculate Conception of the Blessed Virgin Mary (8 December), Entrance Antiphon.

[144] *Ibid.,* Preface.

[145] *Liturgy of the Hours,* Solemnity of the Immaculate Conception of the Blessed Virgin Mary (8 December), Midafternoon, Reading (Eph 5:25-27).

48. Today, theological reflection on Mary's Immaculate Conception would do well to deal with the challenges posed to the dogma defined by Pius IX, for example, its relation to the doctrine of original sin, which, while rejecting the most radical contemporary position which denies the existence of any sin, is today the object of a far-ranging hermeneutical investigation.

Mary's Immaculate Conception is a forceful sign of God's grace operative within a creature: Gift of the Trinity's love, this grace allowed Mary, with her liberty rooted in grace, to live her life of freely welcoming love without limit.

The doctrine means that the Virgin of Nazareth fulfilled in herself the human condition which God wished: She was a woman oriented toward that which was on high, not bent over by the weight of sin; she was not enclosed in herself but open to the love of God, to the love of humanity, to the love of creation; she was not a slave signed with the mark of mankind's enemy, but was the beloved daughter of the Father[146] who, from the beginning of her existence, had "the seal of God on [her] forehead" (Rv 9:4: cf. 7:3).

The doctrine means that Mary, the one woman in history with an undivided heart and free from inner discord, presents in a vivid and distinct manner the hope of humanity as it searches for a future of peace, justice, harmony, and community.

The doctrine means that the Mother of Jesus is the mirror of the two dimensions of existence. The Virgin, although full of grace (cf. Lk 1:28), was not exempted from the human condition of suffering, darkness, inner struggle, and sorrow. As disciple, Mary had to grow in faith, to overcome in hope difficult trials, to direct her virginal love to God, to Joseph of Nazareth, to her Son Jesus, to the ecclesial community, to all men and women, her brothers and sisters. But it also means that Mary presents the truest and most beautiful form of human existence, free from

---

[146] *LG*, 53.

deception and turmoil; bright with the splendor of truth and goodness; radiant with the beauty of harmony and perfection, simplicity and transparency.

The Gift and Sign of the Glorious Assumption of the Mother of God

49. Mary's Assumption into heaven is an event which is clearly part of salvation history, a gift of God and a sign of grace for the Church and for men and women of our time. While not considering for the moment the opportuneness of the dogmatic pronouncement made while Christianity was in a state of division, the definition of Pius XII (1 November 1950) confirmed a doctrine on the final destiny of the Virgin Mary which was sufficiently developed and professed by the Church even before the sad division between Constantinople and Rome (1054) and also the divisions which developed in the West in the sixteenth and seventeenth centuries.

The definition of Pius XII reads: "...by the authority of our Lord Jesus Christ, of the Blessed Apostles Peter and Paul, and by our own authority, we pronounce, declare, and define it to be a divinely revealed dogma that the Immaculate Mother of God, the ever-Virgin Mary, having completed the course of her earthly life, was assumed body and soul into heavenly glory."[147] The definition of 1 November 1950 brought great joy to the Catholic Church, but was a grave disappointment to the Orthodox and Protestants. The definition raised much contention in ecumenical circles.

50. The challenge presented by the doctrine of Mary's Assumption to Catholic theology is today particularly difficult,

---

[147] *AAS,* 42 (1950), 770.

not only because of the precise object of Pius XII's definition, but also because of the numerous implications it has for eschatology, a section of theology brimming with developments, not all of which are shared by theologians nor harmoniously integrated into the Church's perennial teaching. However, the Catholic theologian cannot bypass the fact of the dogmatic definition of Pius XII by emptying it of meaning; nor can the theologian withdraw from dealing with the numerous problems which the definition must confront. We will now mention a few.

The Death of Mary

Tradition commonly spoke of the death of the Mother of Jesus. Still Pius XII wished to leave out of the defining formula the question of her death. With that decision he seemed at the time to strengthen "the immortalist movement," which still exists although it has lost much influence. In fact, the hypothesis that the Virgin did not suffer death cuts into the parallelism between the redeeming Son and the mother, which was invoked to strengthen, because of its relation to other revealed truths,[148] the doctrine of the corporal glorification of Mary.

The Assumption of the Mother of Jesus is essentially an

---

[148] "...which is completely in harmony with the other revealed truths (*ceteris revelatis veritatibus summer consona*)," *ibid*, 769; cf. n. 147, www.ewtn, 41. In a catechesis of 25 June 1997, John Paul II authoritatively interpreted the meaning of the circumlocution "having completed her earthly existence (*expleto terrestris vitae cursu*)," in place of the simpler expression "after her death." John Paul II observes: "Pius XII did not intend to deny the fact of her death, but merely did not judge it opportune to affirm solemnly the death of the Mother of God as a truth to be accepted by all believers. Some have maintained that the Blessed Virgin did not die and was immediately raised from earthly life to heavenly glory. However, this opinion was unknown until the 17th century, whereas a common tradition actually exists which sees Mary's death as her entry into heavenly glory." The pope, however, did not conceal his position in favor of the death of the Virgin: "...Since Christ died, it would be difficult to maintain the contrary for his mother." John Paul II, *Theotókos: Woman, Mother, Disciple: A Catechesis on Mary, Mother of God* (Boston: Pauline Books & Media, 2000), 200.

event of a grace including, as was the case for Jesus, both a *death* and a *Resurrection* (not to be understood simply as a reanimation of a corpse but as a creative act of God) of which the modality is not known. Most theologians, including John Paul II, teach that Mary died a "natural death."[149] Still the question of "natural death," considered from the viewpoint of the attitude with which Mary accepted death, is compatible both with the notion of *dormition*, typical of the Eastern liturgies, and of a "death of love," of which some mystics and theologians speak.

The Nature of the Privileges of the Assumption

In the bull *Munificentissimus Deus*, the Assumption of Mary is referred to many times as a privilege,[150] as "the supreme culmination of her privileges,"[151] yet, the term *privilege* is not found in the words of definition. In this regard, some theologians hold that the Assumption does not consist in the corporal glorification of Mary since all faithful are called, in the divine plan, to be glorified in their body and in their soul, either at the end of time in the parousia or immediately after their death according to those who favor a *Resurrection in death*, a theory which cannot be absolutely excluded since it corresponds to the

---

[149] "As to the cause of Mary's death, the opinions seem groundless that wish to exclude her from death by natural causes. It is more important to look for the Blessed Virgin's spiritual attitude at the moment of her departure from this world. In this regard, St. Francis de Sales maintained that Mary's death was due to a transport of love. He speaks of a dying 'in love for her Son Jesus' (*Treatise on the Love of God*, bk. 7, ch. 13-14). Whatever from the physical point of view was the organic, biological cause of the end of her bodily life, it can be said that for Mary the passage from this life to the next was the full development of grace in glory, so that no death can ever be so fittingly described as a 'dormition' as hers." *Ibid.*, 202.

[150] Cf. *AAS* 42 (1950), 754, 756, 758, 759, 762, 769.

[151] *Ibid.*, 768; www.ewtn.com, 40.

corporal glorification in heaven.[152] In this perspective, Mary's Assumption prefigures in a singular way the future of the Church on earth, and it personifies the unique way of the Church in heaven, including its cosmic and social relationships (cf. Rm 8: 19-25). Still a peaceful perusal of the theological traditions of East and West, especially of the texts of the liturgy, leads to the following two conclusions:

— first, the event of the Assumption deals with the *body* of Mary, the virginal dwelling place for the Incarnate Word which, according to the *sensus fidei,* could not undergo the corruption and dissolution of death,[153] and was, in a way we know not, transported into heaven.[154]

— second, in the full and perfect glorification of the totality of her being, Mary *anticipates* the future of all of the redeemed: In her Assumption, the Virgin *is already* that which the Church "herself desires and hopes wholly to be."[155]

As regards the theory that the just "rise in death" and therefore all "those who die in Christ" have attained their final state,

---

[152] Theologians refer to Enoch, who "walked with God and was no longer, because God had taken him" (Gn 5:24; cf. Sir 44:16; Heb 11:5), and to the prophet Elijah (cf. 2 K 2:1; Si 48:9), and they point to Judaism's tendency to assign a similar fate to the great personages of Israel: the patriarchs Abraham, Isaac and Jacob, Moses, Baruch and Ezra; and, in the New Testament, to the martyrs in the Book of Revelation 6:9-11.

[153] See the well-known collect, *Veneranda,* found in the *Sacramentarium Gregorianum "ex authentico"* (J. Deshusses, *Le sacramentaire gregorien: ses principales formes d'apres les plus anciens manuscrits* [Fribourg: Editions Universitaires, 1971, no. 661, Vol. I, 262-263]) and cited in *Munificentissimus,* in *AAS* 42 (1950), 59.

[154] "As the most glorious Mother of Christ, our Savior and God and giver of life and immortality, was endowed with life by him, she has received an eternal incorruptibility of the body together with him, who has raised her up from the tomb and has taken her to himself in a way known only to him" (*Encomium in beatam Virginem,* 14: *PG* 86, 3312). This *Encomium,* once attributed to Saint Modestus of Jerusalem [† 634], is found in the works of an anonymous author who lived at the end of the eighth or at the beginning of the ninth century.

[155] *SC,* 103.

the magisterium has several time emphasized that the case of Mary was altogether unique,[156] and the Church underscores the importance of the "last day" (cf. Jn 6:39-40, 44, 54; 11:24), the parousia of Christ, when the Resurrection of the dead will occur (cf. 1 Cor 15:20-28); it teaches that there is a period of waiting or of eschatological distance between the moment of death (*here, now*) and the event of the Resurrection of the body (*at the end of time*), which is professed in the creed: "We look for the Resurrection of the dead, and the life of the world to come."[157] Paul VI integrated the Assumption of Mary into the ensemble of the Christian mysteries: "Joined by a close and indissoluble bond to the Mysteries of the Incarnation and Redemption, the Blessed Virgin, the Immaculate, was at the end of her earthly life raised body and soul to heavenly glory and likened to her risen Son in *anticipation* of the future lot of all the just."[158]

The Biblical Foundation

The question of the biblical foundation of the doctrine of the Assumption is another of the "numerous problems" raised by the definition of 1 November 1950. The decisive argument which favored the dogmatic definition of the Assumption of Mary was the witness of the universal consensus of pastors and also of the people, that is, of the universal Church, and its ac-

---

[156] "6. In teaching her doctrine about man's destiny after death, the Church excludes any explanation that would deprive the Assumption of the Virgin Mary of its unique meaning, namely the fact that the bodily glorification of the Virgin is an anticipation of the glorification that is the destiny of all the other elect." Congregation for the Doctrine of the Faith, "Letter on Certain Questions Concerning Eschatology," *OR* (23 July 1979), 7-8. (*Recentiores episcoporum Synodi* de quibusdam quaestionibus ad Eschatologiam spectantibus [17 May 1979] 6); in *AAS* 71 (1979), 941.

[157] Nicene Creed, *DS* 150.

[158] Paul VI, *Solemn Profession of Faith* (30 June 1968), *OR* (11 July 1968), 5. See with the *Catechism of the Catholic Church* (11 October 1992; English translation 1994), 966: "The Assumption of the Blessed Virgin is a singular participation in her Son's Resurrection and an anticipation of the Resurrection of other Christians."

ceptance by the Catholic Church which, infallibly guided by the Spirit of truth (cf. Jn 16:13), recognized as revealed from God a truth which by natural means could not have been known.

But this consensus derived ultimately from the Scripture was also the result of centuries-long meditation on the Word by God's holy people: "By this appreciation of the faith (*sensus fidei*), aroused and sustained by the Spirit of truth, the People of God... receives not the mere word of men, but truly the word of God (cf. 1 Th 2:13), the faith once for all delivered to the saints (cf. Jude 3). The People unfailingly adheres to this faith, penetrates it more deeply with right judgment, and applies it more fully in daily life."[159]

Guided by the Spirit, the faithful have understood that the close and indissoluble bond, attested to by the Scripture, between Christ the Redeemer and his generous associate in the fight against the enemy of the human race, should be continued in their triumph over sin and death (cf. Gn 3:15). In other words the Resurrection of the Son should include something comparable for the mother — an Assumption into heaven. The Virgin "was taken up body and soul into heavenly glory, when her earthly life was over, and exalted by the Lord as Queen over all things, that she might be the more fully conformed to her Son, the Lord of lords (cf. Rv 19:16), and conqueror of sin and death."[160]

In *Munificentissimus Deus,* Pius XII did not indicate any specific biblical text in favor of the corporal Assumption of Mary. He preferred to consider revelation as God's communication to humanity in history which has its culminating moment in Christ — his life and death, his words and actions, his Resurrection and its continuation through the Church of his presence in history and in the world. The Old Testament points to Christ

---

[159] *LG,* 12.
[160] *Ibid.,* 59.

and the New begins with him. Pius XII limited himself to giving certain passages which frequently served as starting points for a theological meditation on the Assumption of Mary and were found in both the liturgies of the East and the West for the feast of 15 August. However, by affirming that these truths "are based upon the sacred writings (*quae veritas Sacris Litteris innititur*) as their ultimate foundation,"[161] Pius XII introduced a distinction, often not sufficiently noticed, between the truth *asserted* by the Scripture and the truth which is present in its *inner depth*. Obviously the Assumption belongs to the latter type of truth.

Today, rather than pointing out that the Bible says nothing on the mystery of the Assumption, it seems more important to ask if it is contrary to the Scripture to assert that the Scriptures, in some cases, contain *orientations* which, with the assistance and guidance of the Holy Spirit, can be developed by theological and ecclesial reflection. Today, it is necessary to develop theologically the nature and the value, the limits and the rules governing this *orientation* — this larger reading of the Scripture.

51. The theology of the Assumption is particularly complex and difficult. Still the essential nucleus of the mystery, as it was proposed in the defining formula of *Munificentissimus Deus* and in the commentary of *Lumen Gentium*,[162] is sufficiently clear and shared by theologians with diverse anthropological orientations; namely, having completed her life, the Mother of Jesus was glorified in the totality of her being, rendered completely conformable to the Son, and became the "first fruits" and image of the Church.

---

[161] *Munificentissimus* 13. The same bull refers another time to this affirmation: "All these proofs and considerations of the holy Fathers and the theologians are based upon the Sacred Writings (*Sacris Litteris, tam quam ultimo fundamento, nituntur*) as their ultimate foundation. These set the loving Mother of God as it were before our very eyes as most intimately joined to her divine Son and as always sharing his lot" (*ibid.*, 38).

[162] *LG*, 59 and 68.

Today, theological reflection, observing the similarity found in Genesis 3:15, John 2:1-5, and Revelation 12:1, sees the event of the Assumption as *sign*[163] and strives to discern its multiple significance.

Sign of a Destiny of Glory

After the resurrected Christ, the Virgin's Assumption is a sign of dignity of persons — male and female — and of their future destiny to glory. Both events — the Resurrection of Jesus and the Assumption of Mary — teach us that the destiny of humanity, made to the "image and likeness" of God (cf. Gn 1: 26-27), is not an undoing of personhood and a dissolution into nothingness, but the full realization and total conformity to Christ, by having arrived to "the full stature of Christ" (cf. Eph 4:13), or, as the East prefers to say, to "divinization." Closely united to her Son and member of the heavenly Jerusalem, the Blessed Virgin is deeply immersed in the trinitarian life: She is closely united with Christ and she points out to the numerous band of saved individuals the *space* — the humanity of Christ — of their inclusion into the divine, into the life and the mercy of the Father, into the light and wisdom of the Son, into the radiant love of the Holy Spirit. Mary, in her glorification, is the sign of the completion of the human vocation, the only one who fulfills this vocation: to be enveloped in the glory of the living God, to resonate the hymn of pure praise, and to respond in pure love.

---

[163] In the Apostolic Exhortation *Signum Magnum* (*SM*) (13 May 1967), Paul VI observed, "The great sign which the Apostle John saw in heaven, 'a woman clothed with the sun' [Rv 12:1], is interpreted by the sacred Liturgy, not without foundation, as referring to the most blessed Mary, the mother of all people by the grace of Christ the Redeemer." *TPS* 12:3 (1967), 278; *AAS* 59 (1967), 465.

The ways of God are not our ways (cf. Is 55:8). According to the account in Genesis, God made the human body — male and female (cf. Gn 1:26-27; 2:7, 21-23), the work of his hands. In his infinite goodness and wisdom, according to the Trinity's design, the Father decreed that the Son, in the fullness of time (cf. Gal 4:4), become man and take a true human body from the woman Mary of Nazareth.

Rejecting every temptation to docetism, the Church has always upheld the reality of the Incarnation of the Word. In the Virgin's body the Word was conceived in his human nature; she bore him within her during her pregnancy, she gave him birth, she nursed him. The presence of the Holy One of God made the body of Mary "the habitable dwelling space" of the Word; for that reason, Christian devotion, through the figure of "promise-completion" (*umbra-veritas*), has applied to Mary ancient Israel's highest cultic symbols referring to the God who lived in the midst of the people and accompanied them on their journey, namely, the *ark,* the *cloud,* the *tent,* the *temple,* the *holy of holies.* But above all, this presence of the Savior within Mary has made Mary's body a "space of salvation," because God has freed his people from sin "in the mysteries of his flesh,"[164] making it the "hinge" of salvation. In the celebrated phrase of Tertullian, "the key is the salvation of the flesh (*caro salutis est cardo*),"[165] but that flesh is the flesh taken from Mary; as the striking phrase from the patristic era states, "the body of Christ, body of Mary."

The Incarnation of the Word and the Assumption of the Virgin have saved the human body and, in particular, the fem-

---

[164] *LG,* 55.
[165] *De Resurrectione mortuorum* VIII, 2: CCL 2, 931. On Tertullian, see Luigi Gambero, *Mary and the Fathers of the Church: The Blessed Virgin Mary in Patristic Thought.* Trans., Thomas Buffer (San Francisco: Ignatius Press, 1999), 61f.

inine body, from the disdainful way it was considered in many sectors of the ancient world.

The Incarnation of the Son of God in the body of a woman was considered aberrant, unthinkable, unworthy of God. The Christian faith in the Resurrection of the body was also rejected as being a "hope befitting worms."[166] In the salvific design of God, the Incarnation of the Word was the highest expression of God's love manifested in an unprecedented *kenosis* (cf. Ph 2:6-8), in which, in a totally different way, the mother also participated. God's *foolish love* for humanity had decreed that, in the humiliation of the Incarnation, there came the triumph of the Resurrection and the glory of the Assumption.

Women who look to the Virgin in her Assumption see a person whose dignity has been restored, whose body, frequently the object of profanation, has been made holy, a body which has integrated the value of the feminine into the mystery of God. Because women know that the gift given by God to Mary is destined to be shared by all women, Mary's sisters, this contemplation of Mary's body is a joyful portent of their own future dignity.

The Beginning and Eschatological Image of the Church

The Church has not here a lasting city (cf. Heb 13:14), but it is always a people on journey toward its fulfillment which will take place only in the glory of heaven, when, "together with the human race, the universe itself, which is so closely related to man and which attains its destiny through him, will be perfectly reestablished in Christ (cf. Eph 1:10; Col 1:20; 2 P 3:10-13)."[167]

---

[166] Origen, *Contra Celsum* V, 14: *SCh* 147, 48.
[167] *LG,* 48.

Mary's Assumption is part of God's salvific plan and it has profound christological and ecclesial implications. In *Munificentissimus Deus,* Pius XII outlined the christological aspects, and, Vatican II, the ecclesial aspects. Theological reflection of the past decade has begun to develop the ecclesial dimensions of the Assumption.

In relation to the Church, the Virgin assumed into heaven is:

— The *beginning* of the Church both in a theological and in a chronological sense. Mary is the member of the Church perfectly redeemed; in her, "the Church has already reached that perfection whereby she is without spot or wrinkle (cf. Eph 5:27)"[168]; she is the virgin through the integrity of her faith, the bride resplendent in beauty through her intimate union with Christ, the mother who has given birth to numerous children born at the baptismal font "by water and Spirit" (Jn 3:5); she is holy through the presence in her of the Spirit of Holiness; in relation to the other members of the Church, Mary is the first disciple who has journeyed the entire pilgrimage of faith[169] and has participated fully in the paschal mystery of Christ; she is the first member of God's royal and priestly people (cf. 1 P 2:9), and, seated at the throne of the Most High, she has entered heaven's sanctuary to unite her voice of supplication to that of Christ, our Eternal High Priest, who lives forever to make intercession for us (cf. Heb 7:25).

— As eschatological *icon,* the image of the *assumpta* shines before the pilgrim Church on earth. Mary is that human creature who has arrived at the fullness of her divine vocation, the prototype of the eschatological Church; the

---

[168] *Ibid.,* 65.
[169] *RM,* 25-26.

icon of the *assumpta* is not static but has a drawing power; it not only presents an image of aesthetic enjoyment, but it is also a synthesis of the divine plan which God, through Christ in the Spirit, has made and continues to make possible to save humanity; and it is above all an impetus and stimulus to advance quickly on the path traced out by God for reaching the salvific future promise.

Sign of Sure Hope and Comfort

With the Scriptures, the Church proclaims that Christ alone is our supreme hope, the "hope for glory" (cf. Col 1:26-27); still it recognizes other signs of hope and of consolation which the Lord has placed along its path, especially that of the Mother of Jesus. In this regard Vatican II stated, "The Mother of Jesus, glorified in body and soul in heaven… shines forth on earth, until the day of the Lord shall come (cf. 2 P 3:10), a sign of certain hope and comfort to the pilgrim People of God."[170] Behind these words are centuries of ecclesial experience, expressed in metaphors by theology and devotion, which are still fitting: for example, the experience of one's own condition, as part of a people *on journey* traveling through an arid desert toward the promised land; the experience of sailors who in the darkness of night find themselves in a boat being tossed in a stormy sea; the experience of the maternal intervention of Mary who points to all generations that Jesus is the way, the truth, and the life (cf. Jn 14:6) and who in the darkness of history shines as the star of the sea (*maris stella*)[171] directing sailors toward Christ, their secure and final resting place.

---

[170] *LG,* 68.

[171] *Liturgy of the Hours,* Common of the Blessed Virgin Mary, Evening Prayer II, "Ave Maris Stella," author unknown, attested to in the 9th century; cf. Bernard of Clairvaux, *In laudibus Virginis Matris* II, 17; *SBO* IV, 34-35.

The Church of heaven and the Church on earth are not two different realities but two stages of the same mystery. There is communication between these two periods. The members of the heavenly Church intercede for men and women still subject to the dangers of earthly existence; the members of the Church on earth venerate their brothers and sisters already arrived at their heavenly goal and, in particular, they praise "Mary, the ever-virgin mother of Jesus Christ our Lord and God"[172] and they join with her in the liturgy of praise. The primary position which the Mother of God occupied in the community praying in the Cenacle (cf. Ac 1:12-14) is prolonged in the sanctuary in heaven. Through her perfect glorification, through her close union with her Son, which made her "spiritual body" (cf. 1 Cor 15:44) no longer subject to vicissitudes of time and space, Mary is the meeting point for those who dwell in heaven and those who dwell on earth; hers is the totally pure hymn of praise, hers is the most efficacious prayer; she is the benign and maternal presence which brings about in the community of disciples growth toward a greater fraternity and family. In a discreet manner, she is present to the Church where her Son, the High Priest, the only Master and Lord, dwells; she is the sign that the liberation of the cosmos (cf. Rm 8:19-22) has already begun, because "in the glorified body of Mary, material creation begins to share in the resurrected body of Christ."[173]

---

[172] *Roman Missal,* Eucharistic Prayer I, Roman Canon.

[173] Third General Conference of the Latin American Episcopate, *Evangelization in Latin America's Present and Future* (Puebla de los Angeles, 1979), in Gary MacEóin, *Puebla: A Church Being Born* (New York: Paulist Press, 1980), 163-164.

Sign of God's Manner of Acting

Observing the interventions of God in history, theologians have noted a continuity in his way of acting: "a divine style" derived from the divine action. A sure part of this divine style is a predilection for the little ones and the humble: "The Lord raises the needy from the dust, lifts the poor from the ash heap, seats them with princes, the princes of the people" (Ps 113:7-8; cf. 1 S 2:8; Ps 107:41). He directs his countenance toward "the lowly and afflicted man who trembles at [his] word" (Is 66:2). That is why he looks upon the humble servant, Mary of Nazareth, who proclaimed, "he has looked upon his handmaid's lowliness" (Lk 1:48) — the humility of heart and the humility of her social condition — and she concludes, "The Mighty One has done great things for me" (Lk 1:49). The Assumption of Mary is the final result of God directing his countenance to his lowly servant and it well illustrates the words of the Lord, "the one who humbles himself will be exalted" (Lk 14:11; 18:14). Mary humbles herself as she identifies herself, in all honesty and in accord with Israel's finest tradition, to be the "servant of the Lord" (Lk 1:38); therefore, in accord with God's style, she is raised on high (cf. Mt 23:12).

The Assumption of Mary is the emblematic symbol of God's way of acting: The Virgin of Nazareth, an insignificant creature in the eyes of the world, has become, through God's grace, the most important person in history and in eternity.

52. Holy Church honors the Blessed Virgin as the mediatrix[174] "through whom we have received the author of life."[175] John Paul II interpreted the Church's tradition on this point as he spoke of the intervention of the mother with her Son at the marriage feast of Cana (cf. Jn 2:3) as the first manifestation of "the mediation of Mary" which "with this character of 'intercession'... continues in the history of the Church and the world."[176] The principle enunciated at Vatican II that "the unique mediation of the Redeemer does not exclude but rather gives rise to a manifold cooperation which is but a sharing in this one source"[177] is especially applicable to the Virgin Mary.

Today, many theologians, with a commendable intention of deepening and making this doctrine more precise, speak of the mediation of Mary from different points of view and in new terms. Many of the aspects of the doctrine of Mary's mediation — its nature, its scope, and its relation with other forms of subordinate mediation — are disputed among theologians, for which reason a renewed and more profound study of these questions is necessary.[178] We believe that such a study should not be undertaken with the intention, terminology, and images used by many theologians before Vatican II, but rather that the orientation and directives outlined in *Lumen Gentium*[179] be

---

[174] *LG*, 62; *Masses*, 30. "The Blessed Virgin Mary, Mother and Mediatrix of Grace."

[175] *Roman Missal*, Mary, Mother of God (1 January), Opening Prayer.

[176] *RM*, 40.

[177] *LG*, 62.

[178] In this regard the Pontifical International Marian Academy published the following statement in *The Declaration of the Theological Commission of the Pontifical International Marian Academy* (August 1996): "Even if the titles were assigned a content and could be accepted as belonging to the deposit of faith, the definition of these titles, however, in the present situation would be lacking in theological clarity, as such titles and doctrines inherent in them still require further study in a renewed Trinitarian, ecclesiological, and anthropological perspective" (*OR* [4 June 1997], 12).

[179] *LG*, 62.

followed. John Paul II has often considered the cooperation of the Virgin in the Trinitarian salvific plan under the terms "the mediation of Christ" and "maternal mediation," that is, as one aspect of Mary's universal motherhood in the order of grace.[180] Many theologians regard this context for studying Mary's mediation as a profitable one, based on sound biblical foundations (cf. Jn 19:26-27), in accord with the *sensus fidelium,* and less subject to controversy.

The "Marian Dimension" of the Christian Life

53. Doctrine and devotion are the areas in which many wish to consider the Mother of the Lord. In *Redemptoris Mater,* John Paul II made reference to a theme which, although it has much in common with Marian doctrine and devotion, is innovative, that is, "Marian spirituality" or, as some prefer, "the Marian dimension of Christian spirituality."[181] After having extended an invitation to "promote a new and more careful reading of what the Council said about the Blessed Virgin Mary,"[182] John Paul II added:

> Here we speak not only of the *doctrine of faith* but also of the *life of faith,* and thus of authentic "Marian spirituality" seen in the light of Tradition, and especially the spirituality to which the Council exhorts

---

[180] *RM,* Part III, Maternal Mediation, see 38-47.

[181] The two expressions are acceptable: the first, "Marian spirituality," used many times by John Paul II, is simpler and indicates the specific dimension — the Marian — which it intends to describe; the second, "Marian dimension of Christian spirituality," is more complex, but it has the advantage of highlighting that there is *one Christian* spirituality, capable of further definition as a result of historical experience, and to point out that *Christian spirituality,* which has its origins in Christ and constantly refers to Christ, has in itself an essential, not optional, *Marian dimension.*

[182] *RM,* 48.

us. Furthermore, Marian *spirituality*, like its corresponding *devotion*, finds a very rich source in the historical experience of individuals and of the various Christian communities present among the different peoples and nations of the world.[183]

John Paul II's invitation is motivated by the lack of dialogue between dogmatic theology and ascetical theology, between mariology and Marian spirituality. This lack of dialogue can be seen in the theologies of various cultures and in various theological approaches.

Christian spirituality is essentially one: It is life in the Spirit (cf. Gal 5:18) and animated by the Spirit (cf. Rm 8:2-14), which unites us to Christ and progressively conforms, transforms, and transfigures us to him (cf. Rm 8:29; 2 Cor 3:18), bringing to completion our status of being adopted children of God the Father (cf. 1 Jn 3:1-2; Eph 1:5; Jn 1:12). Life in the Spirit of Christ has its beginnings in baptism and is lived in and through the Church. Christian spirituality is trinitarian, ecclesial, sacramental. Here the question spontaneously arises: What role has the Virgin Mary in this process which transforms the disciple into "another Christ"? What are its biblical-theological foundations? How is it expressed?

John Paul II has given some directives for studying this question. He indicated that this "Marian dimension" is a personal bond, derived from the maternal-filial bond, which is established between the Mother of Jesus and each of his disciples and constitutes "a unique and unrepeatable relationship."[184] He outlined the fundamental meaning of "the words spoken by Jesus to his Mother at the hour of the Cross: 'Woman behold your son' and to the disciple: 'Behold your mother' (Jn 19:26-27). They

---

[183] *Ibid.*
[184] *RM*, 45.

are words which determine Mary's place in the life of Christ's disciples"[185] and give "the reason for the Marian dimension"[186] of Christian life and spirituality. The relation between Mary and every disciple of Christ has a gratuitous character — a pure gift: "The Redeemer entrusts his mother to the disciple, and at the same time he gives her to him as his mother. Mary's motherhood which becomes man's inheritance is a gift: a gift which Christ himself makes personally to every individual."[187] The terms "entrustment" and "welcome acceptance," both derived from biblical terms, express the profundity of this relationship:

> Such entrusting is the response to a person's love, and in particular to the love of a mother. The Marian dimension of the life of a disciple of Christ is expressed in a special way precisely through this filial entrusting to the Mother of Christ, which began with the testament of the Redeemer on Golgotha. Entrusting himself to Mary in a filial manner, the Christian, like the Apostle John, "welcomes" the Mother of Christ "into his own home" and brings her into everything that makes up his inner life, that is to say, into his human and Christian 'I': he "took her to his own home."[188]

54. The reasons advanced by theologians to include the "Marian dimension" as an intrinsic element of "Christian spirituality" are many:

— Mary's *essential role* in relation to Christ of whom she is the true mother according to human nature and the generous

---

[185] *Ibid.*, 44.
[186] *Ibid.*, 45.
[187] *Ibid.*
[188] *Ibid.*

cooperator (*generosa socia*) in the work of salvation[189];

— her *spiritual maternity* to the disciples of Jesus to whom she brings the life of grace, nourishing and educating them until they have arrived to perfect conformity with Christ; hers is a true maternity "in the order of grace,"[190] which cannot be reduced to an accessory role;

— her *maternal queenship* in relation to the Church and to individual disciples; her queenship is based on Jesus, not on the ways of the world (cf. Jn 18:36); it is a queenship consisting in the service of love, the expression of mercy, and constant intercession[191] so that all of the disciples of Jesus and all people redeemed by him might "inherit the kingdom prepared... from the foundation of the world" (Mt 25:34);

— her *exemplary value* which presents the virtue and the attitudes which constitute the basis for "Christian spirituality" as found in the Gospel[192]; here the Virgin is the model of filial love for God the Father, of a profound communion with Christ, and of docile assent to the voice of the Spirit;

— her *multiple relations* to the Church, of which she is its final pattern (*simillima*)[193]; here, as some theologians have pointed out, is the basis for the Church's "Marian profile" of which the spousal dimension is one part;

— her *constant memory* which the Church invokes in the liturgy, not only recalling the sacred events in which she

---

[189] Cf. *LG, 61.*
[190] *Ibid.*
[191] Cf. *CMBVM,* 39, "Holy Mary, Queen and Mother of Mercy," Entrance Antiphon.
[192] Cf. *MC,* 57; *CMBVM,* General Introduction, "The power of Mary's example in celebrations of the liturgy," 14-18.
[193] Augustine, *Sermo 213 (In Traditione Symboli),* 8: *NBA* 32/1, 212.

participated, but celebrating the divine mysteries with her and in her spirit of worship.[194]

The essential attitude, which constitutes "Marian spirituality," flows from the close relationship between the Mother of the Lord and the disciples, and involves a trinitarian, ecclesial, and sacramental perspective directed toward attaining perfect love for God and neighbor (cf. Mt 22:34-40; Mk 12:28-31), and it is lived consciously and perseveringly. Insofar as Marian spirituality is rooted in the "event of Christ," it precedes in a certain sense the "mystery of the Church" and has priority over other spiritualities which have developed in the course of centuries, for instance, monastic and Franciscan spiritualities, which of their nature can not be universal nor obligatory.

55. Mary of Nazareth is the universal model of the Christian life and discipleship. Every disciple of the Lord is influenced by Marian spirituality. From a historical point of view, Marian spirituality flourished in ascetical groups or, as we today say, in institutes of the consecrated life.

Here John Paul II well stated the common teaching: "The relationship with Mary most holy, which for every believer stems from his or her union with Christ, is even more pronounced in the life of consecrated persons [...] Mary's presence is of fundamental importance both for the spiritual life of each consecrated person and for the solidity, unity and progress of the whole community"[195]

---

[194] "When the liturgy turns its gaze either to the primitive Church or to the Church of our own days it always finds Mary. In the primitive Church she is seen praying with the apostles; in our own day she is actively present, and the Church desires to live the mystery of Christ with her" (*MC,* 11, 16-20); "In union with the Blessed Virgin and in imitation of her reverent devotion, the Church celebrates the divine mysteries by which 'God is perfectly glorified and the participants made holy'" (*CMBVM,* General Introduction, 13).

[195] John Paul II, Apostolic Exhortation *On the Consecrated Life. Vita Consecrata* (25 March 1996), 28, in *AAS* 88 (1996), 401; in *Origins* 25:41 (1996), 681-719.

56. In the course of the centuries Marian spirituality has taken various forms derived from theological and cultural developments of various periods, and from some aspect or role of the Mother of the Lord which is to be highlighted. Here we will outline a few of these forms.

Imitation. This involves the recognition of an exemplary value, unique and universal, of the Blessed Virgin in relation to a life of genuine discipleship; this imitation, lived in conscious awareness of the Virgin's quiet sanctity, leads the disciple to know more profoundly the person of Mary and her mission, to imitate her Gospel virtues, and to progress without interruption on the road to holiness.[196]

Historically, proposing the Mother of Jesus as the model for the Christian life had its beginnings in ascetical circles of women. From the third century, eminent theologians like Origen († 253) proposed to consecrated virgins the figure of Mary of Nazareth as the foremost model of Christian virginity.[197] After him, in the fourth and fifth centuries, the great teachers of the spiritual life and pastors such as Saint Athanasius († 373), Saint Gregory Nazianzen († 390), Saint Gregory of Nyssa († 392), Saint Ambrose († 397), Saint Jerome († 419), and Saint Augustine († 430) developed a solid theology of the relations

---

[196] In our time the Church's magisterium, liturgical theology, and teachers of spirituality have developed well the reflection on Mary's exemplarity. For the teaching of the magisterium: *LG*, 65-67; *SM*; *MC*, 57; *RM*, 42-44. For the testimony of the liturgy, see the noteworthy synthesis of the efficacy of Mary's exemplarity in the liturgical action: "The powerful example of Mary that shines out in the celebration of the liturgy urges the faithful to become like the Mother, in order that they might be fashioned more completely in the likeness of her Son. Her example also prompts the faithful to celebrate the mysteries of Christ with that same spirit of reverent devotion with which she took part in the birth of her Son, in his epiphanies, and in his death and Resurrection. In particular, Mary's example urges the faithful: to treasure the word of God in their hearts and dwell upon it assiduously; to praise God exultantly and thank him joyously; to serve God and neighbor faithfully and offer themselves generously; to pray with perseverance and make their petitions with confidence; to act in all things with mercy and humility; to cherish the law of God and embrace it with love; to love God in everything and above everything else; to be ready to meet Christ when he comes." *CMBVM*, General Introduction, 17.

[197] Cf. *Commentarii in Matthaeum X*, 17: *SCh* 162, 216.

between consecrated virgins and Mary who was proposed as *model* of virgins and *mirror* of every virtue.[198]

It is the task of mariology to give close attention to the exemplary value of Mary's holiness for all the Christian people. The model which she offers should not be understood as an ideal and static point of reference, removed from the actual life-situation of the Christian people, but as a source of inspiration, providing many fruitful ways in which her spirit of dedication is applicable to various situations.

Service. The trait is derived from the awareness of the transcendent dignity of Mary, Lady and Queen, because she is the Mother of Christ, the Lord and the King of Glory (cf. Ps 23 [24]:8; 1 Cor 2:8). It consists in giving oneself to her — freely, totally, lovingly, and happily — in order to serve the Lord and one's neighbor more perfectly and to enjoy the protection of our Lord and our Lady in time of danger.

This trait of Marian spirituality was found in the East from the end of the sixth century; in the West a forceful proponent of service in imitation of Mary was Saint Ildephonsus of Toledo († 667) who saw its foundations in the divine maternity, its purpose in the more perfect service of God, its fruits in the nobility of spirit which led to the acquisition of genuine liberty and to confidence of salvation.

From the eighth to the thirteenth centuries there were several saints and ecclesiastics who professed themselves to be servants of the glorious Virgin Mary, among whom were Pope John VII († 707), who called himself the servant of holy Mary (*servus sanctae Mariae*)[199]; Alcuin († 804), who had a decisive influence on the cultural renewal which occurred in the Carolingian lands; Saint Fulbert of Chartres († 1028); Saint Odilo of Cluny († 1049), who has left us the oldest formula of

---

[198] Cf. Athanasius of Alexandria, *Epistula ad virgines*: CSCO 151, 59-62.
[199] Text in H. Leclercq, *Forum chrétien: DACL* 5/2, 2016-2018

"profession of service" yet discovered[200]; Saint Peter Damian († 1072), whose Marian devotion and doctrine strongly influenced the eleventh century; the great Saint Bernard († 1153), who, to express his intimate sentiments for Mary, *Domina Mundi* (Ruler of the World) and the *Regina Caeli* (Queen of Heaven), placed himself as an unworthy servant before a glorious and compassionate lady; the Seven Holy Founders of the Servants of Mary (Servites), who, "for the honor of God placed themselves at the service of the Virgin Mary and from that moment wished to be called the Servants of Holy Mary,"[201] in order that the glorious Virgin, mediatrix and advocate, might reconcile and recommend them to her Son. In the same centuries, reflection on service (*servitus, mancipium*) to the Virgin developed. Based on the examples provided in Scripture, such as the mysterious figure of the "Servant of Yahweh" (cf. Is 42:1-4, 49:1-6, 50:4-9, 53: 12-53:13), of Mary of Nazareth "servant of the Lord" (Lk 1: 38), of Paul "a servant of Jesus Christ" (Rm 1:1), the biblical foundations of Marian service were harmonized with more local observances derived from feudal ceremonies which sanctioned the relations between the lord (*dominus*) and the servants of the manor; these expressions were then found in the literary genre of "courtly love" and of chivalry. There were many witnesses who expressed the joy and the honor of serving the Queen of Heaven, confident of her assistance to free them from the slavery of sin and to assist them to advance in the way of virtue.

Consecration

Already John Damascene († 749) refers to Marian consecration which is a total gift of self — mind, soul, body, one's

---

[200] Text in Jotsald, *Vita Odilonis* II, 1: *PL* 142, 915-916.
[201] *Legenda de origine Ordinis,* 18, in *Monumenta OSM* I, 74.

whole person — to the Mother of God, together with a consciousness of her presence.[202] Gradually consecration became an important part of Marian spirituality. In the eighteenth century, Saint Louis Marie Grignion de Montfort († 1716) gave a christological and baptismal dimension to Marian consecration.[203] At the present, the concept of consecration to the Blessed Virgin has been an object of an ongoing analysis and reflection. Here we note that there appears in the texts of John Paul II an increasing preference for the term *entrustment*.

Oblation

This trait of Marian devotion was associated with the Marian sodalities and lay movements originating in the seventeenth century, usually with the encouragement of the Society of Jesus. The notion of oblation was inspired by the Virgin's fiat (cf. Lk 1: 38) in the mystery of the Annunciation-Incarnation; it involves the recognition of the Mother of God as the Lady, patroness, advocate, and exemplary model of the Christian life; it is expressed in the "offering to Mary," prompted by love, "in union with her," as the way of living one's fundamental consecration to God within the Church.

---

[202] John Damascene, *Homily I on the Dormition,* 14, *PG* 96, 720 C-D; the first part of this extract is in *Mary and the Fathers,* 404: "We today also remain near you, O Lady. Yes, I repeat, O Lady, Mother of God and Virgin. We bind our souls to your hope, as to a most firm and totally unbreakable anchor, consecrating to you (*anathémenoi*) mind, soul, body.... With what happiness, and how blessed is the one who has made his intellect a storehouse for your sacred remembrance."

[203] Cf. St. Louis Mary de Montfort, *True Devotion to Mary.* Translated from the original French by Françoise de Castro (Bay Shore, NY: Montfort Publications, 1955). Montfort's title was "Act of Consecration to Jesus Christ, the Incarnate Wisdom, by the Hands of Mary," *The Love of Eternal Wisdom* [Trans., A. Somers, S.M.M.], (Bay Shore, NY: Montfort Publications, 1960), 124-126.

Slavery

This trait of Marian devotion arose at the end of the sixteenth century in the Franciscan circles of Alcalá of Henares, and was propagated by leading teachers in the seventeenth century.[204] The devotion of slavery was well accepted in France by eminent saints and spiritual teachers[205] and after that in all of Europe. Slavery expressed in a radical way the free offering of one's self and one's liberty to the Mother of God "without any limits, except the commandments of the God of infinite majesty,"[206] as Venerable Henri-Marie Boudon wrote. The teaching on slavery had a strong theocentric orientation encouraging its followers to divest themselves of the old person and to put on the new.

The Marian-Centered Life (*Vita mariaforme*)

In the seventeenth century, there arose in the Carmelite family a new expression of Marian spirituality. This Marian style of life arose from the mystical experience of Marie Petyt († 1667), a Carmelite tertiary, and was promoted by the Venerable Michael of Saint Augustine († 1684) in his treatise *De*

---

[204] "Marian slavery" was never associated with one religious family. Although it arose in Franciscan circles favoring the Immaculate Conception, various individuals promoted it: the Trinitarian, Saint Simon of Rojas († 1624), founder of the "Congregation of the Slaves of the Sweet Name of Mary"; the Mercedarian, Peter of Jesus Mary Serna († 1642); the Augustinian, Bartholomew de los Rios († 1652), author of *The Slave of Mary* and promoter of the Marian slavery in Belgium (in 1641, he published at Antwerp his famous work, *De hierarchia mariana,* in which several times he refers to the dignity of being a slave of Mary).

[205] Among these leaders are Louis Jobert († 1719), Jesuit, author of the volume *La dévotion du saint esclavage de la Mère de Dieu,* published at Paris in 1668, at the same time that Henri-Marie Boudon († 1702) published *Dieu seul. Le saint esclavage de l'admirable Mère de Dieu*; the famous Cardinal, Pierre de Bérulle († 1629), founder of the French school of spirituality of the seventeenth century, who pronounced a vow of slavery to the Mother of God; and Saint Louis Marie Grignion de Montfort († 1716) who, through the clarity of his writing, the sound foundation of his teaching, and the holiness of his life contributed to the acceptance of the notion of Marian slavery.

[206] H.-M. Boudon, *Oeuvres complètes,* a cura di J.-P. Migne, II, Paris 1856, 379.

vita mariaeformi et mariana in Maria propter Mariam, written first in Flemish (1669), then in Latin (1671). This Marian-centered life, possible only with the help and guidance of the Holy Spirit, consists in joining one's filial love for God with a filial love for the Virgin Mary, in which the disciples "use the same measure for determining that which is conformable with the will of God and that of the admirable Mother. In all matters of discernment, they strive to have their eyes fixed on God and on his most holy Mother."[207] To "live *in* Mary" means that "in our actions, in our sufferings, in what we do and what we do not do, in our afflictions and trials, we strive to develop and to nourish within us a filial, tender, innocent orientation of the heart, a vital, animated love for Mary as mother most amiable and beloved by God."[208] To "live *through* Mary" means "to devote all our energies to her service, honor, and love, in order that she may be honored, glorified and loved in all things, and that her reign advance and reach perfection in the kingdom of her Son Jesus."[209]

Spirituality of the Heart of Mary (Cordimarian Spirituality)

In the nineteenth century, through Saint Anthony Mary Claret († 1870), cordimarian spirituality arose, with a distinct filial, apostolic, and missionary emphasis, by which the members of the Claretian family live their Christian life, their eyes on the Immaculate Heart of Mary, symbol of her person and her

---

[207] *De vita mariaeformi et mariana,* chap. 1. Michele de Saint'Agostino. *Vita mariaforme.* Italian version of Ignazio del Bambin Gesù (Rome: Edizioni Monfortane, 1982), 31. Cf. José Maria Hernández Martinez, English of *Ex Abundantia Cordis: A Study of the Cordimarian Spirituality of the Claretian Missionaries* (Rome: Secretariat of the Heart of Mary, 1991).

[208] *De vita,* chap. 2, 34.

[209] *Ibid.,* chap. 4, 39.

interior life, of her fidelity to the word of God, and to the action of the Holy Spirit.[210]

Filial Love and the Alliance with Mary

The essential points of the Marian spirituality of Blessed William Joseph Chaminade († 1850), founder of the Society of Mary (Marianists), are *filial love* and *alliance with Mary.* In the relation of filial love between Mary, our true mother, and her true children (not simply adopted children), Chaminade introduced an original perspective: the responsibility of loving the Virgin Mary with the same love with which Jesus loved her; *filial love* then is the prolongation of the love which Jesus had for his mother. In the *alliance with Mary,* Chaminade used the biblical categories which dealt with the covenant (cf. Ex 19:5-6) to express the relation between Mary and her true children: They have chosen Mary, their sovereign, as their mother, and she has chosen them as her special family (*familia peculiaris*).[211] The alliance then is the result of a free and enduring choice made by Mary and by her children. For that reason Marianist religious profess the "vow of stability" which places them "permanently and irrevocably in the state of a servant of Mary,"[212] and they are dedicated to apostolic activity intended to bring about the kingdom of Christ and to make Mary better known and better loved.

---

[210] Cf. *Escritos espirituales.* Carta a un devoto del Corazón de María (Madrid, *BAC,* 1985), 497-506.

[211] Cf. G.-J. Chaminade. *Écrits marials,* II (Fribourg, Séminaire Marianiste, 1966), nos. 751-753, 279-281.

[212] *Ibid.,* nos. 578, 212.

Characteristic of the Marian spirituality of Saint Teresa Benedicta of the Cross (Edith Stein), the Carmelite martyr of Auschwitz († 1942), was *Marian accompaniment (chiragogia)*. The presence of Mary was a part of Edith Stein's life, especially after her entry into Carmel. She knew the lines of Carmelite Marian spirituality in which the Virgin is mother, queen, and sister to every member of the Carmelite family. Important to her were Mary's spiritual maternity, her espousal, her exemplarity. Rather than contemplate Mary as a model, which implied a certain distance and an impossibility of attaining the ideal, Edith Stein preferred an 'accompanying presence,' that is, a hand-in-hand journey with Mary to Christ. This is the Marian spirituality of Edith Stein: to trust in the direction of the Virgin, to place oneself under her guidance, to allow oneself to be led by her hand.[213]

57. Contemporary ecclesial movements, many of which are composed predominantly of laity, with a significant apostolic dimension, have an explicit Marian spirituality. Thus the *Schoenstatt Work,* founded by Joseph Kentenich († 1968), defines itself as an apostolic Marian movement, dedicated to Mary, Mother Thrice Admirable, Queen, and Victress. The Marian spirituality of the Schoenstatt Work consists in the covenant of love which the Christian seals with Mary, certain that with her help and in imitation of her virtues the Christian may embark upon the way which leads to a fuller union with Christ and, through Christ under the influence of the Spirit, to communion with the Father: *"Per Mariam ad Iesum, per Iesum cum Maria in Spiritu Sancto ad Patrem"* is the formula which well expressed the nucleus of the Marian spirituality of the Schoenstatt Work.

---

[213] Cf. Edith Stein, *Die Frau: Ihre Aufgabe nach Natur und Gnade* (Louvain: Nauwelaerts, 1959).

The *Militia of the Immaculata,* founded by Saint Maximilian Kolbe († 1941), the heroic martyr of faith and charity killed in the Auschwitz concentration camp, is a strongly Marian apostolic movement. The Militia emphasizes the mystery of the Immaculata which, in the theological outlook of Kolbe, constituted her essence, the root of her person and action: Mary is the Immaculata, the Immaculata is Mary. The dominant note of the spirituality of the Militia is total consecration to the Immaculata in which the knights ask the Virgin to accept them as her "property and possession" and to make of them and of all their faculties of mind and body, of their "life, death, and eternity," whatever would be pleasing to her.[214] It is an act of love and "knightly service," of which the external sign is the Miraculous Medal. As the movement progressed, Kolbe's consecration to the Immaculata assumed some mystical elements: "The Immaculata — Here is our ideal. To draw near her, to become like her, to permit that she take possession of our heart and of our whole person, that she live and work in us and through us, that she even love God with all our heart, that we belong to her without any reservation — this is our ideal."[215]

With an intentionally Marian title, *The Work of Mary* is the name of the large and complex *Focolare Movement* which began at Trent in 1943, founded by a lay woman, Chiara Lubich. In Focolare, the Holy Family of Nazareth — a family of lay persons dedicated to the service of God and of neighbor (neither Joseph, Mary, nor Jesus belonged to a class of consecrated persons according to the Jewish law) — constitutes the necessary point of reference for every *focolare,* because each *focolare* is to make present the reality of the house of Nazareth:

---

[214] *Scritti di Massimiliano Kolbe,* "Atto di consacrazione alla B.V.M. Immacolata" (Rome, Enmi, 1997), 2392-2393. English: *Maria Was His Middle Name: Day-by-Day with Blessed Maximilian Maria Kolbe,* excerpts from his writings and addresses selected, compiled, and arranged by Jerzy M. Domanski, ed., translated and with an introduction by Regis N. Barwig (Altadena, CA: Benziger Sisters, 1977).

[215] *Ibid.,* "Il nostro ideale" (24 June 1936), 2117.

two virgins — a man and a woman — with Jesus "in the midst of them" (cf. Mt 18:20). The foundress insisted that, within the movement, Mary be seen as a 'lay' person so as to attract and to amaze the contemporary world: "...Jesus and Mary: the Word of God, the Son of a carpenter; the Seat of Wisdom, the mother of the house."[216] A characteristic of the movement is to see the struggles of the Church and of the world through the eyes of Mary — which leads to an intense desire for the unity of Christians and for sharing the many sorrows of humanity. "Live Mary" is another Focolare expression: It means to quiet our inner self in order to hear, with Mary, the voice of the Spirit; to dwell on the virtues of Mary, to continue her mission of giving Jesus to the world.

58. This survey, though incomplete, shows that the ecclesial awareness of the role of Mary in the disciple's spiritual life is ancient, universal, and part of the experience of men and women noted for the holiness of their lives. This experience should be considered a gift of the Spirit for the life of the Church.

At the beginning of the third millennium, when theologians, members of institutes of consecrated life and the laity have a deep interest in spirituality, it seems a favorable moment for an evaluation and for an acceptance of Marian spirituality as a principal element of the Christian life. But as regard some aspects of this spirituality, there may be some hesitations and doubts. We will list a few so that students of mariology will be able to clarify and make any corrections which may be necessary.

Notwithstanding the legitimacy and the usefulness of the expression "Marian spirituality," it seems necessary, by way of introduction or an explanation of terms, to state that it is an intrinsic component or dimension of the one Christian spirituality. On 10 December 1987, John Paul II while listing the tasks await-

---

[216] C. Lubich, *L'attrattiva del tempo moderno*, Scritti spirituali, I (Rome: Città Nuova Editrice, 1978), 27.

ing mariologists said: "In the area of spirituality, which today arouses wide interest, the promoters of mariology should show the need for a harmonious insertion of the 'Marian dimension' into the one Christian spirituality, because it is rooted in the will of Christ."[217] This clarification should overcome the danger of understanding "Marian spirituality" as something which is apart from, or parallel to, Christian spirituality.

For some exegetes and theologians, the parameters of the following terms are not clearly defined: *doctrine* or the biblical-theological reflection on the Virgin Mary; *devotion* or the acts and practices with which she is venerated; and *spirituality* or the way to live the Christian life in which the Blessed Virgin plays a significant role. Does not the study of Scripture and Tradition — they assert — furnish the elements of Marian spirituality? Are not the acts of devotion — liturgical or popular — rich expressions of that spirituality? In other words, this preoccupation to define the "epistemological composition" of Marian spirituality appears excessive to them.

It is not easy to determine exactly where Marian spirituality fits into the panorama of theological disciplines. The question arises of where it should be located: In mariology — because it refers directly to Mary of Nazareth? In christology — because it is one of its intrinsic dimensions? In the history of spirituality — because the varied expressions of Marian spirituality are part of a well-defined historical context in light of which these can be more easily understood? In ecclesiology — because authoritative authors have insisted that "Marian spirituality in its precise sense is identical with ecclesial spirituality"[218]? But others counter that ecclesial spirituality is liturgical spirituality, whose center is the celebration of the paschal mystery.

Contrary to those who consider the variety of expressions of

---

[217] John Paul II, "Address to the Pontifical Theological Faculty 'Marianum,'" 4, in *AAS* 81 (1989), 774; *OR* (16 January 1989), 6.

[218] Hans Urs von Balthasar, *Il Vangelo come norma e critica di ogni spiritualità nella Chiesa*, in *Concilium* 1 (1965/4), 83.

Marian spirituality unfortunate, we believe that they are inspired by the Spirit and that they have been profitable for the Church's life. In the expressions of devotion, we must avoid the danger of falling either into narrow parochialism, an impoverished and limited approach to the mystery of Mary, or of overvaluing some expressions, putting them, more or less consciously, into the category of being ends in themselves. Similarly, we should avoid trying to reconcile expressions which are inexact or not justified with other expressions of Marian spirituality. Let us avoid the controversy, never entirely settled, over whether the interior life is superior to the liturgy as the means to arrive at the experience of God.

Genuine expressions of Marian spirituality, faithful to their charisms, are open to the great principles of Christian spirituality: namely, (1) the essential value of the Word of God for acquisition of Wisdom and knowledge of God's plan (cf. 1 Tm 2:3-4); (2) the celebration of the liturgy instituted by Christ as the memorial of his paschal mystery (cf. 1 Cor 11:23-26), where the disciple is truly and progressively transformed into Christ and reaches the source, Christ's Spirit, and becomes a child obedient to the Father cleansed from all sin; (3) the way of the cross, the indispensable means of becoming a disciple (cf. Mt 16:24; Mk 8:34; Lk 9:23); (4) docility to the voice of the Spirit who lives in the heart of the disciple and teaches him about the life of grace (cf. Rm 8:1-17); (5) love for the Church, the first sign of the kingdom, where every member is a citizen of God's household and family (cf. Eph 2:19) and rejoices in Christ's love as spouse (cf. Eph 5:25-27; Gal 2:20); (6) a great desire for the unity of the Church (cf. Jn 17:11, 20-22).

In each of these "means and principles" the Virgin Mary is present. The varied expressions of Marian spirituality attempt to highlight an aspect of the active presence of the Mother of the Lord without, however, obscuring the others or distracting the disciple from contemplating the totality of the mystery of Mary.

Observations on Vocabulary

— We wish to encourage the efforts made, frequently by institutions which are directly involved, to avoid the danger of certain expressions which cast a negative light on some forms of Marian spirituality, for example, the term 'slavery,' used to indicate a total dedication of the faithful to Mary, or words such as 'thing,' 'property,' 'instrument' to indicate, in some contexts, men and women who have become slaves of Mary. These terms are hard to reconcile with contemporary culture and hardly consonant with human dignity;

— We encourage the request which many theologians have made for the last several years for a more careful use of the expression *"consecration* to Mary." Strictly speaking, consecration, inasmuch as it is a free, total, irrevocable, and perpetual donation, is directed toward God alone. The expression 'consecrated to Mary' is, however, acceptable in reference of the institutes of consecrated life or of approved pontifical ecclesial movements when their dedication is an integral part of their formula of membership or profession. However, the term *consecration* appears 'inappropriate' in other situations, for example, those in which children and families are entrusted to Mary's protection.[219]

---

[219] See the Congregation for Divine Worship, *Orientations and Proposals for the Celebration of the Marian Year 1987-1988* (3 April 1987), 86: "The word *consecration,* when it refers to persons, has the idea of totality and perpetuity of the gift of self to God, as can be seen by its deep roots in the field of worship. But in the pastoral situation of shrines it is used in a wide sense and incorrectly: for example, people talk of 'consecrating children to the Blessed Virgin,' when, in reality, what is intended is only to place the children under the protection of the Blessed Virgin and to ask her motherly blessing for them. The consecration to the Blessed Virgin — of families, parochial groups, or parishes, just on the spot, for example, on a visit to a shrine — must not be the fruit of a passing emotion, as sincere as it may be. Such consecration requires personal decision, made freely and maturely after reflection. This must start from a correct evaluation of the primary and fundamental consecration at baptism, and must reach an exact understanding of the theological meaning of consecration to Mary."

— We should take care that expressions of Marian devotion do not give the impression, many times denounced, that the works of grace proper to the Holy Spirit are now entrusted to Mary. For example, the progressive transformation of the faithful into Christ is essentially the work of the Holy Spirit; however, the Virgin Mary, remaining within the limits of her sphere of action, acts in union with the Spirit. This terminology comes from the Baroque period, and it would be well to avoid it.

By Way of Conclusion

59. The existence of a "Marian spirituality" is an indisputable part of the Church's life. But, so that its nature and its characteristics may become clearer, it is necessary: (1) to undertake the study of the origins, the historical developments, of its structure and its theological contents; (2) to clearly state that it is a dimension or aspect of the one Christian spirituality; (3) to highlight the trinitarian horizon in which "Marian spirituality" is found, and, in particular, its profound pneumatological dimension; (4) to purify the language where necessary; (5) to avoid any one-sided approach and to overcome the tendency toward division within the ecclesial community.

Again, by way of conclusion, we submit a text of the Congregation for Catholic Education which, without resolving all the questions, offers a synthesis of the problems related to Marian spirituality and provides a way for a deeper understanding.

The study of mariology holds as its ultimate aim the acquisition of a sound Marian spirituality, an essential aspect of Christian spirituality. On his pilgrim way to the measure of the stature of the fullness of Christ (Eph 4:13), knowing the mission which God has entrusted to the Virgin in the history of salvation and in the life of the Church, the Christian takes her as "mother and teacher of the spiritual life" [cf. *MC,* 21; *CMBVM,* "Mother and Teacher in the Spirit"]; with her and like her, in the light of the Incarnation and of Easter, he impresses on his very existence a decisive orientation towards God through Christ in the Spirit, in order to express by his life in the Church the radical message of the Good News, especially the commandment of love (cf. Jn 15:12).[220]

The Presence of Mary in Christian Morality

60. Jesus is the center, the norm, and the goal of our moral striving. He is the way which leads to our ethical perfection, the truth which enlightens with his splendor the life to which every man and woman aspires (cf. Jn 14:6). Jesus is also the one who reveals and teaches the new law: He faithfully fulfills the will of the Father (cf. Lk 2:49; Jn 8:29; Mt 6:10; 26:39) and lives in the Trinity's reciprocal love (cf. Jn 13:34; 15:12, 17), always ready to bestow life on us (cf. 1 Jn 3:16).

Viewed in this christological light, the figure of Mary has attracted, more than in the past, the attention of moral theologians. In manuals of moral theology there was no place for the Virgin Mary, although they may have tried to see Mary in the first precept of the Decalogue dealing with the divine worship, or the second commandment dealing with blasphemy. Various causes have contributed to this increasing interest of moralists in the Virgin Mary:

---

[220] *VMISF,* 36.

— the convergence in moral theology and in mariology of the importance of the dignity of human persons; moral theology underlines the primordial importance of persons — their dignity and liberty, their conscience and responsibility — through the ethical evaluation of human acts. In mariology, Mary is presented as the highest expression of the *human person* through her ability, lived with liberty and responsibility, to relate to God the Father, with whom she has entered into a profound and salvific dialogue; to the divine Son with whom she has shared in a unique way human life and the paschal mystery; to the Holy Spirit to whose interior movements she has docilely responded; to the ecclesial community to which she has transmitted her exceptional testimony regarding the words and the events surrounding Jesus' infancy (cf. Lk 2:19, 51) and with whom in the Cenacle she awaited the coming of the Spirit (cf. Ac 1:14).

— the progressive revelation of the *exemplary value* of the life of the immaculate Mother of God,[221] through which she is a "radiant sign and inviting model of the moral life,"[222] whose "sublime virtues... attract souls in an irresistible way to imitation of the divine model, Jesus Christ, of whom she was the most faithful image,"[223] or as the suggestive metaphor of Theodore the Studite († 826) puts it: "She is the sacred book of the commandments of the Lord, the law of grace — now written, through which we know what is pleasing to God."[224]

---

[221] *MC*, 57.

[222] John Paul II, *Veritatis Splendor,* Encyclical on the Splendor of Truth (6 August 1993), 120 in *Origins* (14 October 1993), 297-336; cf. *LG*, 65.

[223] Paul VI, Apostolic Exhortation *On Venerating and Imitating the Virgin Mary, Mother of the Church and Model of All Virtues. Signum Magnum* (13 May 1967), I, in *AAS* 59 (1967), 469.

[224] *Omelia sulla dormizione della Madre di Dio* 4, 10: *PG* 99, 725.

— the increasing attraction for the ancient title addressing the Virgin Mary as the *Mother of Life*[225]: the Mother of Christ who is the Life (cf. Jn 11:25; 14:6) is also the Mother of the living (cf. Gn 3:20), of those reborn by the baptismal waters. In response to the tragic incursion of the culture of death, Mary appears as the eminent figure of the culture of life: she is the first who, welcoming the message of the angel (cf. Lk 1:26-38), received the Gospel of life in its primordial and fundamental form — Jesus; bearing the life within her, she assisted Elizabeth, her cousin, as that elderly woman gave birth to the precursor (cf. Lk 1:39-58); together with Saint Joseph she was guardian of life against the fury of the powerful ruler (cf. Mt 2:13-23); she recognized the inestimable value of the water and blood which flowed from the pierced side of Christ (cf. Jn 19:34), "the font of life" according to the interpretation of the mystics[226] and when, standing at the foot of the cross, she gave testimony of his life-giving death.

— the increasing awareness in the Church that the Virgin Mary has *a formative role in Christian morality.* She is not only a model, but, as mother, she takes part in the moral education of her children and accompanies them on the path of their moral transformation. She is the fulcrum of Christian morality: in contemplating her person, human and Christian dignity appear in its fullness. She witnesses to the transforming power of grace which is offered and communicated to us in Christ; she teaches that true life is not a 'saving' but 'losing' of oneself for the sake of Christ (cf. Mt 16:25) and in the service of our brothers and sisters.

---

[225] Germanus of Constantinople, *Omelia I sulla dormizione della Madre di Dio: PG* 98, 348; in *Mary and the Fathers,* 389.
[226] Cf. Bonaventure of Bagnoregio, *Lignum vitae,* 29-30.

Here are points of great value for moral theology. They require a deeper investigation and clarification, but we can comprehend the great benefits which can be derived from them. In moral theology, the figure of Mary will never more be considered as marginal; rather, she will be a strong point of reference in the moral formation of the disciples of Christ.

The Presence of Mary in the Social and Political Sphere

61. Reflection on the "presence" of Mary in social and political spheres began in the twentieth century. However, the influence of the Church's constant teaching on Mary of Nazareth in the social and political arenas of the 'human city' is ancient, present already in the patristic era.

This phenomenon is very complex, requiring much historical research and a quiet calm evaluation of the data which emerge. Here we wish to provide to students of mariology, without any pretence of being complete, some considerations to give direction to the discussion.

The influence of Mary on the social and political sphere has a twofold origin:

— The *Virgin herself who,* although she lives outside of history, has not renounced her salvific mission[227] and has assumed a personal initiative;

— The *disciples of the Lord* who, while contemplating the figure and the mission of Mary, decide to commit themselves to social action promoting solidarity and the progress of people.

---

[227] Cf. *LG,* 62.

62. With her Assumption into heaven of the totality of her being — body and soul — Mary of Nazareth and the activity to which she dedicated herself was completely received by God, transformed in glory, removed from the temporal, the spatial, and the limits of her earthly condition. Through the mystery of the Assumption, Mary is present in a definitive manner to God and also present to the world in a new way. The unbreakable bond of mother and Son, through which she cooperated while on earth in the saving work of Christ,[228] not only is continued in heaven but is also strengthened in a way we cannot describe. The liturgy uses the ancient expression "seated at the side of" to indicate the participation of Mary in the power of her Son:

> Conqueror of the primordial sin and of death,
> mindful of us you are seated beside Christ,
> earth and heaven proclaim you
> queen and powerful one.[229]

The mystery of the Assumption is the point, the *perpetual today,* from which the Virgin Mary "reigns with Christ forever."[230] But her queenly power is uniquely the *power of being compassionate,* the unlimited possibility of offering to those who invoke her true mercy and compassion.[231] It is a service to men and women still exposed to the dangers and perils of earthly existence, and, in the style of God, it is an ear attentive to hear the cry of the oppressed (cf. Ex 3:7; Nb 20:16; Jb 34:28), an eye looking to see the sufferings of her children (cf. Tb 3:3, 15;

---

[228] Cf. *SC,* 103; *LG,* 53.

[229] *Liturgy of the Hours* (Italian version), Assumption of the Blessed Virgin Mary (15 August). Lauds, hymn *Solis, O Virgo, radiis amicta,* 2nd stanza. The hymn is the work of Vittorio Genovesi († 1967).

[230] *Ibid.,* Evening Prayer II, Antiphon, for the *Magnificat.*

[231] Cf. Riccardo di San Lorenzo, *De laudibus beatae Mariae Virginis, IV.* Douai, 1625, 288.

Ps 137 [138]:6; Is 66:2; Lk 1:48). In prayerful intercession to her Son and with her Son she lives as a suppliant on our behalf (cf. Heb 7:25). Her participation in the reign of the resurrected Christ offers the Virgin optimal conditions for carrying out her motherhood of all people. "Glorious in heaven, she [Mary] is at work on this earth."[232]

The personal intervention of the assumed one on earth looks principally, but not exclusively, at the supernatural life of her children, because "while earthly progress must be carefully distinguished from the growth of Christ's kingdom, to the extent that the former can contribute to the better ordering of human society, it is of vital concern to the Kingdom of God."[233]

On earth Mary belonged to the faithful remnant, the "poor of Jahweh," the first among them:[234] "In their hearts they suffer the servitude to which the 'stiff-necked' people are reduced because of their sins. They endure persecution, martyrdom, and death; but they live in hope of deliverance."[235] The Blessed Virgin, personifying this hope, crosses the threshold of the Old Testament,[236] and "in the Magnificat she presents herself as the model for all those... who do not passively accept the adverse circumstances of personal and social life and who are not victims of alienation, as the expression goes today, but who instead join with her in proclaiming that God is the 'avenger of

---

[232] Puebla, 288.

[233] *Gaudium et Spes*, 39. "This hope does not weaken commitment to the progress of the earthly city, but rather gives it meaning and strength. It is of course important to make a careful distinction between earthly progress and the growth of the kingdom, which do not belong to the same order. Nonetheless, this distinction is not a separation; for man's vocation to eternal life does not suppress but confirms his task of using the energies and means which he has received from the Creator for developing his temporal life." (Congregation for the Doctrine of the Faith, Instruction *Libertatis conscientia,* Instruction of Human Freedom and Liberation (22 March 1986), 60, in *AAS* 79 (1987), 579; in *OR* (14 April 1986), 5.

[234] *LG*, 55.

[235] *Libertatis conscientia*, 47.

[236] Cf. *Ibid*, 48.

the lowly' and will, if need be, depose 'the mighty from their thrones'."[237]

In heaven, the Virgin Mary, because she acts in and with Christ, provides for the spiritual needs of those who invoke her, but she is also interested in their temporal needs. She knows that the Christian people, in their confidence, constantly call upon her. Among these requests are those related to peace, to social justice, to the progress of the nation, to the preservation of liberty and human dignity, to the struggle against misery and hunger, and to advancing human culture. In relation to these, the Mother of God also intervenes in a manner not known to us.

The apparition of the Virgin, 12 December 1531, on the hill of Tepeyac to Juan Diego, representative of a 'conquered people,' and through him to Bishop Zumárraga, representative of the better part of the 'conquistadors,' constituted a 'political intervention,' in the highest and noblest sense of the term, in favor of an indigenous people who were the object of aggression. At the same time, the intervention was an evangelical message of fraternity directed to the two peoples, inviting them to renounce violence and to look toward a future with the prospect of entering into a higher cultural synthesis. Four centuries later, the Latin American episcopate acknowledged that, in Guadalupe, "Mary has also been the voice urging us on to union as human beings and as peoples."[238]

The Influence of the Disciple of the Lord

63. But the influence of *doctrine* about Mary on the social and political spheres also includes the path which the disciples of the Lord take.

---

[237] *Puebla*, 297; John Paul II, *Homily at the Sanctuary of Zapopan* (30 January 1979), *OR* (19 February 1979), 3.
[238] *Puebla*, 282.

The disciples of Christ, above all, sense the necessity of harmonizing the situation of citizenship in the temporal city with the awareness that there is not here a permanent dwelling place (cf. Heb 13:14); each is to be "the disciple who builds up the earthly and temporal city while being a diligent pilgrim towards the heavenly and eternal city; the disciple who works for that justice which sets free the oppressed and for that charity which assists the needy; but, above all, the disciple who is the active witness of that love which builds up Christ in people's hearts."[239]

The political and social commitment of the disciples of the Lord is based on faith and on the need to make incarnate the Gospel in the society in which they live. The disciples should animate the secular society with Christian principles; above all, "the lay faithful *are never to relinquish their participation in 'public life,'* that is, in the many different economic, social, legislative, administrative and cultural areas, which are intended to promote organically and institutionally the *common good.*"[240] From a Gospel viewpoint, 'political power' must be an expression of service (cf. Mt 21:24-28), a firm and persevering determination to commit oneself to the common good.

Disciples know that the Blessed Virgin Mary had and continues to have a principal role in the history of salvation. Their profession of faith leads the disciples to contemplate the figure and mission of the Mother of the Lord. They note that the figure of the Virgin, as found in the Gospels, is that of a specific woman, someone who is close to them, a sister on the pilgrimage of faith, who experiences the sorrow and the anguish of searching in the distress of long silences and of endless trials. They note the value of her 'presence' in crucial moments of the

---

[239] *MC,* 37.
[240] John Paul II, *Christifideles laici,* on the Vocation and the Mission of the Lay Faithful in the Church and in the World (30 December 1988), 42, in *AAS* 81 (1989), 472; in *OR* (6 February 1989), 1-21.

life of Christ and the qualities of her soul — humble, strong, generous, compassionate — and her concern for the trials of contemporary men and women.[241] From this conviction arises the commitment to social and political action. Here, by way of hypothesis, we ask: How many disciples, contemplating Mary at the foot of the cross of her Son, the Just One unjustly condemned, have decided to dedicate themselves to abolishing the death penalty in order that other mothers will not weep over their innocent children condemned to death? The disciples recognize that judgment over the life and death of a person belongs to the Lord alone.

64. It is said that in our time the Church's teaching on Mary does not have a compelling resonance on the heart. That may be, but such a claim must be verified. It would be a grave error to disregard these teachings, part of the secure tradition which the Church possesses, the result of its long journey accompanied by the Holy Spirit. Probably today, it is necessary to ask what meaning these teachings have for our faithful. We need, however, to observe certain methodological premises so that these truths are grounded anew in the fresh and fruitful riverbed of the Scriptures and then plunged into the varied reality of our time and its demands; we follow the style of God, who reveals the secrets of the kingdom to the little ones and hides them from the wise and intelligent (cf. Mt 11:25-26); finally, we move from the Church of the poor (*Ecclesia pauperum*) to the poor of the Lord (*pauperes Domini*) of the twenty-first century.

The results will not be disappointing. Mary of Nazareth, with her Son, is the word which does not pass away (cf. Mt 24: 25); she is the contemporary mother to all her children in every age and on every continent; the woman whose 'interior story' every generation in some way relives; she is the unpredictable woman whose mystery is not fully unveiled, for whom every

---

[241] *MC*, 37.

detail, even the most ordinary, has a hidden significance — the swaddling clothes for the newborn (cf. Lk 2:12), the pair of turtle doves as the offering for the firstborn (cf. Lk 2:24), the wine at the wedding feast (cf. Jn 2:3).

Some episcopal conferences have occasionally compared the truths about Mary with the social and political situation of their communities. For example, the bishops of the Philippines lamented that "We rarely associate devotion to Mary with the social dimension of Christian living." They affirmed that the *Magnificat,* although the "words are not to be interpreted in the contemporary sense of class struggle... point to a reversal of the social order in the Kingdom of God."[242] Ancient Israel considered the poor to be the country's shame, still more, a manifestation of a sick society radically contradicting the will of God. Similarly, behind the misery of the poor of our time are the social sins of the powerful and the rich which even today are denounced in the canticle of the Virgin Mary, reminding us that the Lord will cast down the mighty from their thrones and the rich he will send away empty (cf. Lk 1:51-53).

When dealing with the defense of the unborn, a question of great social relevance, the bishops of the United States pointed out the significance of Elizabeth's words to Mary, "Blessed is the fruit of your womb" (Lk 1:42) which — because of Jesus' identification with the little and helpless ones (cf. Mt 25:40, 45) — "are true in a real sense of every unborn child."[243]

With the clear intention of applying the truth of Mary to the political-social situation of the Christian communities of Latin America and to their nations and their "cultural horizons," the Latin American bishops wrote:

---

[242] Catholic Bishops' Conference of the Philippines, *Ang Mahal na Birhen: Mary in Philippine Life Today. A Pastoral Letter on the Blessed Virgin Mary* (2 February 1975), Manila; in *Marianum* 38 (1976), 433.

[243] United States Catholic Conference, *Behold Your Mother – Woman of Faith: A Pastoral Letter on the Blessed Virgin Mary,* 132 (21 November 1973), Washington, DC: Publications Office.

The Immaculate Conception offers us in Mary the visage of the new human being redeemed by Christ, in whom we find an "even more wondrous" (Opening Prayer for the Nativity of Jesus) re-creation of the Paradise project. Mary's Assumption makes clear to us the import and destiny of the body that has been sanctified by grace. In the glorified body of Mary, material creation begins to share in the resurrected body of Christ. Mary assumed into heaven is the full integrity of humanity, body and soul, now reigning in glory and interceding for those human beings who are wayfaring through history. These truths and mysteries shed bright flashes of light on a continent where the profanation of the human being goes on constantly, and where many curl up in a passive fatalism.

Mary is a woman. She is "blest among women." In her, God dignified woman to unsuspected dimensions. In Mary, the Gospel penetrated femininity, redeemed it, and exalted it. This is a capital importance for our cultural horizon, where the woman should be much more highly valued and where her social roles are now being defined more clearly and fully. Mary is the guarantee of woman's grandeur; she is the example of what being a woman means specifically — of her vocation to be the soul, a self-surrender that spiritualizes the flesh and fleshes out the spirit.[244]

Reflecting on some aspects of the relation between the virginity of Mary and contemporary culture, John Paul II proposed an unexpected 'line of inspiration' to encourage the men and women of our world who are sensitive to political ecology.

---

[244] *Puebla*, 298-299.

The Pope asks:

And I wonder: Does not the virginal character which marks the creation of the human person (cf. Gn 2: 4b-7, 22-23) and his recreation in Christ have some inspiration to offer the *environmental movements* of our time which object to the many forms of violence inflicted on creation, to the erosion of nature and the pollution of the environment?

Above all, the theologian must show our contemporaries that the ideal of the new, perfect man was achieved in Christ Jesus, he is the *Man* (cf. Jn 19: 5). In him God's anthropological plan has reached absolute perfection. Now at the root of Christ — his conception in Mary's womb, and in his birth to definitive life — from the undefiled tomb, there is a "virginal element" which has great import in regard to his being an exemplar for all disciples.[245]

In the origins of Christ — his birth from a virgin and his rebirth to life from an unused tomb — there is always a virginal element. Continuing the reflection of John Paul II, a contemporary document notes that: "Mary of Nazareth never suffered corruption. She never knew any kind of deterioration or pollution. She was the 'undefiled Virgin' in body, heart, and spirit. Creation sees mirrored in her the fullness and harmony to which it aspires."[246]

---

[245] "Studying Mary, We Learn Who Jesus Is," *OR* (10 June 1994), 14; (24 May 1992), 12, in *AAS 85* (1993), 670.

[246] *Servants of the Magnificat: The Canticle of the Blessed Virgin and Consecrated Life,* 210th General Chapter of the Order of Servants of Mary, 108 (Rome: General Curia OSM, 1996), 169.

In the eyes of the disciples of the Lord, the Virgin of Nazareth appears as the symbol of nonviolence, of incorruptibility, of pure integrity; deception never weakened her spirit, infidelity her heart, nor violence her body. Contemplation of the *ever-virgin* (*semper virgo*) elicits sentiments of respect and love for nature. When, as part of the divine plan (cf. Gn 1:28), the disciples render service to the human city, they do it with deference, without intrusion, not inflicting unnecessary suffering nor altering the ecological equilibrium so that, for example, our 'sister water,' having lost its fresh purity, not become a bearer of venom, and that the air contaminated by toxic substances not become unbreatheable, an instrument of death.

65. The nexus between complete teaching on Mary and questions on social and political life is the space where the disciple of Christ becomes involved through personal, cultural, and social commitments. The complete teaching on the Virgin Mary, which is a gift from God, the patrimony of the Church, is the light which illumines the mind of the disciples, warms the heart, and impels them to dedicate themselves to the common good in social and political life. The complete teachings on Mary, which echo the truth of God, of Christ, of the Church, of humanity, are teachings which are closely connected and which illuminate each other without losing their meaning and their persuasive force. The complete teachings about Mary which come from on high and which the Virgin, without retaining anything for herself, quietly places at the service of the salvation coming from Christ, have consequences for human life because they bring the Gospel into the concrete events of everyday life.

66. In our time the popes, bishops, and theologians have frequently spoken of the 'presence of Mary' in the life of the Church, a theological theme with many pastoral implications which engender in the faithful sentiments of consolation and of peace. Paul VI observed: "All periods of the Church's history have benefitted and will benefit from the *maternal presence* of the Mother of God because she will remain always indissolubly joined to the mystery of the Mystical Body, of whose Head it was written: 'Jesus Christ is the same, yesterday and today, yes, and forever' (Heb 13:8)."[247]

The magisterium and theology have characterized this presence in various ways:

— *Maternal:* through this aspect, Mary is present to the Church as "mother of people, and most of all those who believe."[248] "By her maternal charity, she cares for the brethren of her Son, who still journey on earth surrounded by dangers and difficulties, until they are led into the happiness of their true home"[249];

— *Active* and *operative:* this aspect emphasizes Mary's concern. Although her heavenly life is in the Blessed Trinity, she offers a solicitous service of love in favor of all Christ's redeemed people;

— *Praying:* The Virgin assumed into heaven unites with the voice of her Son who lives to make intercession on our behalf (cf. Heb 7:25); her voice is one of supplication and of "glorious intercession"[250];

---

[247] *Signum Magnum,* II.
[248] *LG,* 54.
[249] *Ibid.,* 62.
[250] *Roman Missal,* Common of the Blessed Virgin Mary 1, Opening Prayer.

— *Permanent:* "The Virgin is a permanent presence in the whole reality of the salvific mystery,"[251] and will never detract from but always contribute to the kingdom of her Son (cf. Lk 1:33);

— *Feminine:* In the consciousness of the faithful, Mary as woman "creates the family atmosphere, receptivity, love, and respect for life"[252];

— *Exemplary:* Mary, the Mother of Jesus, full of grace (cf. Lk 1:28) and resplendent with every virtue, shows to the Church the way to perfect communion with her Lord and, by the strength of her example, attracts the faithful to follow Christ;

— *Sacramental:* the presence of Mary points as a sign to a higher reality, to the "maternal features of God,"[253] and to God's infinite mercy;

— *Pneumatic:* the glorified body of Mary, having become "spiritual" (cf. 1 Cor 15:44), permits a presence which is not constrained by physical dimensions — time and space, which are characteristic of earthly existence;

— *Discrete:* the Mother of Jesus lived in the historical situation in which she was part of both ancient Israel and the new People of God, and she fulfills her mission of grace in the company of the Church under the action of Christ and of the Holy Spirit;

— *Singular* and *special:* the presence of the Theotokos — her characteristics, her role, her values — constitute a unique event in the history of salvation.

---

[251] *RM*, 31.
[252] *Puebla*, 291.
[253] *Ibid.*

67. Certainly it is the responsibility of theologians to further describe the nature of the presence of the Blessed Virgin in the life of the Church. Here we wish to call attention to one aspect of that presence which has great theological and pastoral importance: the active presence of Mary in the mystery of Christian worship. If she is truly our mother in the order of grace, it is legitimate to ask: What is her role in the liturgy — in baptism — in which we become adopted children of God? Is not baptism the sacrament recalling the conception of Christ — made possible by Mary's faith and by the power of the Spirit — where the Church and the Virgin Mary appear to act in perfect synergism as the newly baptized, through the baptismal font, truly become children both of the Church and of Mary?

The Commitment to Ecumenism:
An Imperative of the Christian Conscience

68. As students of mariology, we all know how great is the dedication of John Paul II's pontificate to ecumenism: He believes that it is a most serious obligation in his service as bishop of Rome. With the help of the Lord, he has promoted many initiatives to achieve the unity of all the disciples of Christ[254]; among these accomplishments are the "interconfessional dialogues at the theological level [which] have produced positive and tangible results: this encourages us to move forward."[255]

As is well known, between the Catholic Church and the churches and ecclesial communities of the West, there are "con-

---

[254] Sections 41-76 of the encyclical *Ut Unum Sint* (*UUS*) outline the ecumenical activities of the Holy See, frequently achieved in collaboration with the World Council of Churches. The account is extensive and positive, for which the Holy Father did not hesitate to state: "It is the first time in history that efforts on behalf of Christian unity have taken on such great proportions and have become so extensive" (*UUS* 41).
[255] *UUS*, 2.

siderable discrepancies of doctrine… concerning the role of Mary in the work of salvation."[256] In the encyclical, *Redemptoris Mater*, John Paul II has dedicated a section to ecumenism[257] and invited the churches of the East and of the West to pursue the continuing dialog to overcome these differences in doctrine concerning the Mother of the Lord, so that we "together look to her as our common Mother."[258] The students of mariology need to be sensitive to issues in the ecumenical movement which the Holy Spirit has brought forth in order to make progress toward the unity of all the disciples of Christ. Occasionally, some approach the ecumenical movement with reservations, as if it were a threat to maintaining the received doctrine of the Church on the Mother of God. Such fears, in our opinion, are unfounded. Genuine ecumenism does not compromise or change the *depositum fidei* on the Blessed Virgin Mary, but proposes, through shared and sincere study and dialog, to help the brothers and sisters of other Christian confessions to know the full revelation concerning Mary of Nazareth and to ponder their situation in view of our historical and cultural explanation of the image of the Virgin Mary. We believe that it would be a serious disappointment if the current discussions on the Mother of God would be an obstacle to rather than a factor for promoting Christian unity.

69. Relying on the teaching of John Paul II, we believe it opportune to recall some principles and norms which should guide theologians in mariological questions. They should follow the lines traced out in Vatican II's decree *Unitatis redintegratio* and the constitution *Lumen Gentium,* which urge theologians to "carefully refrain from whatever might by word or deed lead the separated brethren or any others whatsoever into error about the

---

[256] *RM*, 30; cf. *Unitatis Redintegratio (UR)*, 20; *MC*, 32-33.
[257] *RM*, 29-34.
[258] *Ibid.*, 30.

true doctrine of the Church."[259] This approach has been followed and developed in consequent documents, such as the *Directory for the Application of Principles and Norms on Ecumenism* (25 March 1993)[260] and the encyclical *Ut Unum Sint* (25 May 1995) — both of which suggest ways for advancing on the road to unity. Specifically, John Paul II has pointed out that among the areas of "need of fuller study" before a true consensus of faith can be achieved is "the Virgin Mary, as Mother of God and Icon of the Church, the spiritual Mother who intercedes for Christ's disciples and for all humanity."[261]

70. In both the Catholic Church and other churches and Christian confessions, there is the shared and well-founded conviction that the full unity of the disciples of Christ will be above all a gift of the Holy Spirit, which we should request with a fervent and humble prayer and conversion of heart: "There can be no ecumenism worthy of the name without a change of heart."[262] This requires that Marian studies:

— avoid long-standing prejudices (through a purification of the historical memory) and eliminate "expressions, judgments and actions which do not represent the condition of our separated brethren with truth and fairness and so make mutual relations with them more difficult"[263];

— earnestly advance the ecumenical dialogue which the Holy See and all of the bishops of the Catholic Church have undertaken with the guidance of the Holy Spirit: "Ecumenical dialogue is of essential importance"[264]; "it

---

[259] *LG*, 67.
[260] *AAS*, 85 (1993), 1039-1119; in *Directory for the Application of Principles and Norms on Ecumenism* (Washington, DC: United States Catholic Conference, 1993).
[261] *UUS*, 79.
[262] *UR*, 7; cf. *UUS*, 15.
[263] *UR*, 4.
[264] *UUS*, 32.

has become an urgent necessity, one of the Church's priorities"[265];

— renounce any "false irenicism," which is completely alien to any genuine ecumenical dialog; the Church's teaching on the Blessed Virgin, both that which has been solemnly defined and that of the universal ordinary magisterium, must be "clearly presented in its entirety"[266];

— refrain from imposing on brothers and sisters not in full communion with the Catholic Church "any burden beyond that which is strictly necessary (cf. Ac 15:28),"[267] a counsel especially applicable to doctrinal matters concerning Mary which are disputed even among Catholic theologians themselves.

— use carefully, with great surveillance, terms and formulas related to the Virgin Mary (purification of language). Words or formulas which are not of ancient provenance or are not accepted by a great number of Catholic theologians do not promote mutual understanding; moreover, they arouse grave uneasiness among our brothers and sisters who are not in full communion with the Church; it is best to use terms which express the doctrine precisely and effectively without allowing the possibility of false interpretations;

— avoid every tendency, true or apparent, which presents the figure of the Virgin Mary in isolation from the ecclesial context; this request made by many Anglican and other theologians is not foreign to the genuine Catholic tradition and is not a diminution of the singular and unique features of the holy Theotokos.

---

[265] *Ibid.*, 31.
[266] *UR*, 11; cf. *UUS*, 18.
[267] *Ibid.*, 78.

In accordance with the conciliar teaching, the Pontifical International Marian Academy has tried to be attentive to ecumenical matters. For many years in the international mariological congresses which the academy has organized, there have been joint sessions characterized by open and sincere exchange which have produced *"ecumenical declarations."* But these meetings at the international congresses are not sufficient; we urge that both the Pontifical International Marian Academy and students of mariology devote greater effort to address the ecumenical question.

Mary of Nazareth and Contemporary Women

71. At its closing, Vatican II (8 December 1965) sent a *Message to All Women.*[268] Since that time, "the feminine question" has often appeared in ecclesial discussion. John Paul II has referred to it in various documents,[269] especially in his apostolic letter *Mulieris dignitatem* (15 August 1988)[270] and in the letter *A ciascuna di voi* (29 June 1995).[271] In these he has pointed out that the Mother of the Lord is for women a sure point of reference for pursuing the arduous path leading to full recognition of their dignity, their rights, their vocation and their fundamental equality with man — in the personal, cultural, social, professional, and political spheres. In Mary there is "a return to that 'beginning' in which one finds the 'woman' as she was intended to be in *creation,* and

---

[268] *AAS* 58 (1966), 13-14.

[269] Cf. John Paul II, Apostolic Exhortation *Familiaris Consortio* (22 November 1981), 22-24; Apostolic Exhortation *Christifideles laici* (30 December 1988), 49-52; Message *All'inizio del 1995,* "Woman: Educator toward Peace" (8 December 1995), in *AAS* 87 (1995), 359-365; Letter *In Honor of Mary* to all the priests on Holy Thursday (25 March 1995), in *AAS* 87 (1995), 793-803.

[270] "On the Dignity and Vocation of Women on the Occasion of the Marian Year" (15 August 1988), in *OR* (3 October 1988); *AAS* 80 (1988), 1653-1729.

[271] "Letter to Women," *OR* (12 July 1995), *AAS* 87 (1995), 803-812.

therefore in the eternal mind of God: in the bosom of the Most Holy Trinity. Mary is 'the new beginning' of the *dignity and vocation of women,* of each and every woman."[272]

In the last decades the commitment of the Church to promote the status of women has been significant, but in the broader context the road to travel is still very long. There are many ethnic groups whose approach to the issue has been locked into rather primitive considerations and deep anthropological judgments which are difficult to overcome.

Some students, motivated by love for the Virgin Mary, the "new woman," have advocated that the principal pastoral responsibility of mariology today should be education directed to the promotion of women. This proposal merits serious consideration.

In the area of doctrine we are happy to note some significant advances:

— new light on certain biblical texts which formerly contributed to interpretations unfavorable to women;

— the recognition that some patristic texts were highly influenced by the situation and culture which existed at the time of their writing;

— the contingent character of many canonical regulations, customs, and liturgical deviations which created, without a valid reason, discrimination against women.

It appears at this point appropriate to repeat what John Paul II stated in his *Letter to Women:* "Transcending the established norms of his own culture, Jesus treated women with openness, respect, acceptance and tenderness. In this way he honored the dignity which women have always possessed according to

---

[272] *MD*, 11.

God's plan and in his love. As we look to Christ at the end of this second millennium, it is natural to ask ourselves how much of his message has been heard and acted upon."[273] Students of mariology should favor the genuine promotion of women, and abandon all perverse apathy so that they may not appear to favor an unjust situation.

72. Students of mariology will also undoubtedly have some reservations about various expressions of Marian devotion. For example, the questions include: What influence did the worship of pagan goddesses have on development of the Church's devotion to the Mother of God? What were the cultural conditions as Marian devotion developed? Were these developments an instrument of ecclesiastical power for keeping women submissive or did they contribute to promoting the dignity of women? There were and continue to be conflicting responses to these questions. We believe that students of mariology should address these and similar questions with an open mind and give an answer which is founded on rigorous and documented historical research.

Inculturation of the Image of Mary

73. The challenge of inculturating divine revelation is ancient, serious, difficult, but *necessary.*

— *Ancient,* because it was already present in the two stages of the Scriptures — Old and New Testaments — and because the Church has had to deal with this challenge in

---

[273] John Paul II, *Letter to Women for Beijing Conference* (29 June 1995), 3, in *OR* (12 July 1995), 2.

every epoch of its history when it wished to preach Christ's Gospel to people of diverse cultures.[274]

— *Serious,* because it deals with essential questions, such as proclamation of the Gospel and the transmission of the contents of the faith which have been defined by councils and other expressions of the magisterium; it touches the worship life of the Church, especially its liturgy,[275] and the daily conduct of Christ's disciples. In his comments on the importance of the relation between faith and culture, John Paul II wrote: "God, revealing himself to the Chosen People, made use of a particular culture: Jesus Christ, Son of God, did the same thing; his human Incarnation was also a cultural Incarnation."[276]

— *Difficult,* because the process of inculturation of the faith requires great wisdom and prudence, discipline and skillful precision — all of which require a profound knowledge of the Church's teaching and an equally profound acquaintance with the culture into which the Gospel message is being transmitted.

— *Necessary,* as stated by Vatican II's *Gaudium et Spes,*[277] by the synod of 1974, dedicated to evangelization, and the synod

---

[274] Cf. *Gaudium et Spes,* 44; Pontifical Biblical Commission, *The Interpretation of the Bible in the Church* (21 September 1993). IV. Interpretation of the Bible in the Life of the Church. B. Inculturation (see n. 48); Congregation for Catholic Education, Instruction *Inspectis dierum* (10 November 1989), 30-32, in *AAS* 82 (1990), 620-622.

[275] Cf. John Paul II, *Vigesimus quintus annus,* 16, in *AAS* 81 (1989), 912-913; Congregation for Divine Worship and Discipline of the Sacraments, Instruction IV. The Roman Liturgy and Inculturation, *Varietates Legitimae,* in *AAS* 87 (1995), 288-314.

[276] John Paul II, *Discourse to University Professors and Men of Culture in Coimbra, Portugal, about the Improvement of Mankind and Cooperation among Peoples through Culture* (1982 May 15), in *OR* (5 July 1982), 6-7; in *Insegnamenti di Giovanni Paolo II* (*Insegnamenti*), V/2 (1982), 1695.

[277] *Gaudium et Spes,* 53-62.

of 1977, on catechetical formation.[278] John Paul II has also spoken about this urgent task: "As she carries out missionary activity among the nations, the Church encounters different cultures and becomes involved in the process of inculturation. The need for such involvement has marked the Church's pilgrimage throughout her history, but today it is particularly *urgent*."[279]

Inculturation includes an examination of many aspects of Marian doctrine. If mariology does not deal with this challenge, the differences between the image of Mary, especially as presented in many outdated cultural expressions, and the images found in contemporary culture, sometimes completely removed from the past, will increase.

It is the challenging and necessary task of mariology "to respond in different historical moments to the demands of different cultures, in order then to mediate the content of faith to those cultures in a coherent and conceptually clear way."[280] It should develop a hermeneutic which is able to express in other cultural settings the doctrine concerning the Mother of God — the truth certain and defined — without losing any of its content, while transcending historical and linguistic limitations.[281]

Such a hermeneutic involves language, content, the existential significance of the doctrine, and should be employed with fidelity to the past, with attention to what is occurring in the present, and with openness to the future. The history of the

---

[278] The themes of the 1974 and 1977 Synods can be found in the Apostolic Exhortations *Evangelii Nuntiandi* (8 December 1975) of Paul VI and *Catechesi Tradendae* (16 October 1979) of John Paul II. The two Exhortations deal with inculturation: *Evangelii Nuntiandi,* 20, 48, 63; *Catechesi Tradendae,* 63.

[279] *Redemptoris Missio,* 50.

[280] *Fides et ratio,* 92.

[281] *Ibid.,* 93.

hermeneutics of Marian doctrine is in many respects exemplary. For example, in proclaiming the Gospel message to people of a polytheistic culture, the Church always insisted upon decisively affirming Mary's human condition. Even when the culture urged people to make of her a goddess, the Church proclaimed that Mary, the daughter of Adam and the humble servant of the Lord, was in God's plan the Theotokos, the all-holy one, who possesses in heaven the great power of intercession.

Today, inculturation includes the challenge of relating Marian doctrine in some way to men and women who live and think in diverse cultural settings. We ought to be trusting and convinced that the reality in the Marian dogmas can be further developed and reformulated, while always being faithful to the sources of revelation and to the dogmatic pronouncements. In turn, the risk of losing or reducing the significance of the Marian doctrines is a reason for going forward with the process of inculturation. If carried out with rigor, there will be a reciprocal enrichment between Marian doctrine and the culture of a people, because "inculturation [is] the Incarnation of the Gospel in native cultures and also the introduction of these cultures into the life of the Church."[282]

---

[282] John Paul II, *Slavorum Apostoli*, 21, in *AAS* 77 (1985), 802.

III

THE VENERATION OF THE MOTHER OF THE LORD

Marian Devotion

74. This letter, addressed to students of mariology, has dealt principally with doctrinal themes. But by way of conclusion, aware that the twentieth international congress, in the year 2000, was both mariological and *Marian*, we would like to say a word about Marian devotion.

Devotion to the Mother of the Lord is a phenomenon with universal dimensions: it is most eminent in the sacred liturgy when "holy Church honors with especial love the Blessed Mary, Mother of God, who is joined by an inseparable bond to the saving work of her Son."[283] The explanation of this phenomenon is not found supposedly in some deviation from the center of Christian worship, but in a modest and progressive consciousness of the role which Mary of Nazareth had and continues to have in salvation history.[284]

The Holy See has provided much direction so that Marian devotion be in harmony with the principles of Christian worship, apart from which it would have no meaning, but within which it forms the most "noble part."[285]

Here we wish only to emphasize that Marian devotion is a form of the "obedience of faith" (cf. Rm 16:26) to the God who reveals. Here are some elements which should be part of sound and integral ecclesial devotion to the one who is *all-holy.*

---

[283] *SC,* 103.
[284] *MC,* Introduction.
[285] *Ibid.*

Accepting the "Gift" of the Mother, an Expression of the "Obedience of Faith"

75. Jesus is the gift of the Father to all humanity: "For God so loved the world that he gave his only Son, so that everyone who believes in him might not perish but might have eternal life" (Jn 3:16). On the Solemnity of Christmas, we sing "For a child is born to us, a son is given us" (Is 9:5).[286] The gift of the Father and of the Son to the Church and to all humanity is the Holy Spirit: "And I will ask the Father, and he will give you another Advocate to be with you always" (Jn 14:16; cf. Jn 14:25, 15:26, 16:7; Lk 24:49; Ac 1:4-5).

The Son and the Spirit, these are the greatest, the ineffable, the unsurpassable gifts of the Father to all humanity. But, in our freedom we have the ability to accept or to reject God's gift. John, the evangelist writes:

> He came to what was his own,
> but his own people did not accept him.
> But to those who did accept him
> he gave power to become children of God,
> to those who believe in his name (Jn 1:11-12).

Among the many gifts with which Jesus, who is one with the Father and the Spirit, has endowed the Church, is his own mother. In John 19:25-27, an episode which exegetes consider as a "revelatory moment," Jesus, dying on the cross, gave his own mother to the beloved disciple and, in him, to all who in faith are his followers.[287]

---

[286] *Roman Missal,* Nativity of the Lord (25 December). Mass during the Day, Entrance Antiphon. Isaiah 9:5 also occurs in the first reading (Is 9:1-3, 5-6) of Mass at Midnight.

[287] *RM,* 23-45, 47; cf. *Roman Missal,* Our Lady of Sorrows (15 September), Opening Prayer.

Mary's maternity in the order of grace is a constitutive element of the saving plan of God, and of his self-revelation in Jesus: To accept this divine revelation is an expression of the "obedience of faith" to God who reveals.

John's Gospel tells us: "This is the work of God, that you believe in the one he sent" (Jn 6:29). We believe in Jesus, in his person, in his word, in his gifts. To accept Jesus means to give honor to the Father who has sent him and made him the way to life (cf. Jn 1:12-13; 17:3). To refuse to accept Jesus, "gift of God," is to offend the Giver of the gift and to enter into the way of death (cf. Jn 8:23-24).

Mary, as mother, is the gift of God and of Jesus to all humanity. To receive this gift, as the beloved disciple did by accepting as his own the Mother of Jesus (cf. Jn 19:27), is a true act of Christian worship because its meaning is drawn from the words of Jesus, "Behold your mother" (Jn 19:27).

In faith and under the inspiration of the Spirit, Mary accepts the word of Jesus on the cross, "Woman, behold your son" (Jn 19:26). In a new way she becomes mother — mother in the order of grace of an immense multitude of children of the Father, brothers and sisters of her firstborn, Jesus (cf. Rm 8:29).

Between the mother and the disciples, in virtue of receiving the gift from Jesus, there is a maternal-filial relationship, "born from the heart of the Paschal Mystery,"[288] which constitutes the essential state of discipleship — the life of grace.

Marian devotion is then an expression of "the obedience of faith" and also involves an awareness of the mother-child relationship which binds the Virgin Mary to the disciples of Christ. Marian devotion, rooted in the paschal mystery, is by nature a significant element of the disciple's life. Here the ancient precept, "Honor your father and your mother" (Ex 20:12),

---

[288] *RM*, 44.

now refers to the disciple's mother in the order of grace; in full conformity with Jesus' teaching, the disciple accepts her with a joyous spontaneity (cf. Lk 2:51). With Saint Anselm († 1109), the disciple astoundingly proclaims: "The Mother of God is our mother."[289] Conscious of the requirements of such a relationship we strive to live in such a way that our conduct truly manifests that we are children of holy Mary.[290]

Marian devotion developed from attentive listening to God's word, guided by the Church under the Spirit's inspiration, and from the acceptance of Christ's paschal gift of Mary as our mother. So that Marian devotion may be a genuine and fruitful expression of Christian worship, it must remain firmly anchored in God's word and in the paschal mystery.

The "Ideal Expression" of Marian Devotion

76. Each of us, students of mariology and pastoral ministers, know how rich, intense, and varied are the expressions of Marian devotion. For that reason, in this concluding section let us outline what appears to us to be the ideal form of Marian devotion.

Marian devotion, because it is drawn primarily from the Scriptures — its message, its words, and its symbols — must have a deep biblical imprint. Its roots are in the Tradition, which is an expression of communion with our predecessors in the faith; it is part of the ecclesial community's collective memory and culture; it is open to renewal and looks toward the limitless horizon which awaits the Christian.

Marian devotion is marked with a deep ecclesial orien-

---

[289] *Oratorio VII.* "Ad sanctam Mariam pro impetrando eius et Christi amore," in M. Corbin, *L'Oeuvre d'Anselme de Cantorbéry* 5 (Paris: Cerf, 1988), 294. Eng. Sr. Benedicta Ward, *The Prayers and Meditations of St. Anselm with the Proslogion* (London: Penguin, 1973), 115-126.

[290] Cf. *Liturgy of the Hours,* Common of the Blessed Virgin Mary, Lauds, Intercessions.

tation: an invitation to communion with the angels and archangels, apostles, martyrs and saints of the heavenly Jerusalem, and with our brothers and sisters of the Church still on pilgrimage here on earth; an open space for sharing their sorrow and anguish, their joys and hopes; a favorable occasion to honor the most eminent member of the Church, the solicitous mother, our sister on the pilgrimage of faith.

Marian devotion is rooted in faith, sustained by hope, lived in charity; it is a devotion in which the liturgy, the sacramental celebration of the saving mystery of Christ with the participation of his Virgin Mother, has the primary role, serving as both the fountain of inspiration and the culmination for all expressions of popular devotion.

Authentic Marian devotion has the following traits:

— *veneration* to the glorious Mother of Christ which ascends in worship and thanksgiving to the very source of Mary's greatness — the Almighty who has done "great things" for her (Lk 1:49);

— *love* toward the Mother of the Living which generates love for our neighbor and, in accordance with the Gospel, even for our enemies and persecutors (cf. Mt 5:43-44; Lk 6:27-28);

— *invocation* of the merciful intercession of the Virgin, which is not enclosed in an individualistic outlook but which is open to the great needs of the Church and world;

— *praise* for the *all-holy one,* accompanied by a commitment to live a life uncompromised with evil, conformable to the Gospel, and mindful of the Lord's monition: "So be perfect, just as your heavenly Father is perfect" (Mt 5:48);

— *wonder* aroused by the contemplation of the pure beauty of the Theotokos which leads to solidarity with the poor, needy, aged and infirm, with those who need bread, lodging, and work.

119

— *imitation* of the Blessed Virgin "who shines forth to the whole community of the elect as the model of virtues"[291] which leads to an increasing transformation[292];

— *loving service* to the compassionate woman and queen of mercy, which invokes the figure of Jesus, "servant of the Lord" (cf. Ac 3:13), who has taken upon himself the sin and sorrow of humanity (cf. Is 53:4-5), which recalls the response of the humble "handmaid of the Lord" (cf. Lk 1:38, 48), and the words of the Master to his disciples: "Whoever wishes to be great among you shall be your servant" (Mt 20:26).

As appropriate for the *tota pulchra,* there is a beauty in Marian devotion, and it should avoid all expressions that are unbecoming and banal. A devotion is beautiful when it arises from a humble and pure heart, simple and sincere; when it is expressed with simple things — paper, cloth, wood (*arte povera*) — tastefully and pleasingly arranged out of love for the Immaculata. It is beautiful when, in homage to Mary, the masterpiece of the Spirit, it brings forth all types of wonderful art, which are extraordinary testimonies of faith and part of the inestimable patrimony given to humanity.

Marian devotion is free from a narrow minimalism which obscures the figure and mission of Mary, and from unbalanced maximalism which leads to false doctrine[293]; it is free from all forms of superstition and from "vain credulity, which substitutes reliance on merely external practices for serious commitment"; it is free from the "sterile and ephemeral sentimentality, so alien to the spirit of the Gospel that demands persevering and prac-

---

[291] *LG*, 65.
[292] *MC*, 57.
[293] *LG*, 67.

tical action"; and which is pure "in its motivation"[294] carefully excluding from the sacred all unworthy self-interest.

Marian devotion balances awareness of the singular dignity and transcendence of the glorious Mother of God with the experience of her closeness to every one of her children because she is in "the Church... the highest after Christ and also closest to us."[295]

Marian devotion welcomes with cordial recognition and with serene liberty the extraordinary manifestations of the Blessed Virgin Mary — apparitions, visions — which are recognized by ecclesiastical authority. They are a sign of motherly compassion, and their 'messages' and 'promises,' often transmitted by humble individuals, can be an encouragement since they are derived from the Gospel and are an extension of the words which the Mother of Jesus addressed at the wedding of Cana, "Do whatever he tells you" (Jn 2:5). They are not meant to be a completion of the Gospel nor a substitute — a type of *easier way*; rather they are intended to awaken within the disciple the necessity of conversion and of following Christ on the royal way of the cross.

Marian devotion reaches its height and becomes a perpetual *Magnificat,* a hymn of pure praise and adoration:

— to the Father, the absolute beginning, the origin of humanity and of the universe, compassionate and "rich in mercy" (Eph 2:4);

— to the Son, the Lord of Glory, the sole Mediator, and the universal Savior;

— to the Spirit, the source of life, the divine fire and wind, the soft breeze.

---

[294] *MC,* 38.
[295] *LG,* 54.

Marian devotion, honoring the Mother, is transformed into the service of humanity, of her children who are subjected to numerous dangers and perils. The glory and purpose of Marian devotion is the adoration of God and salvation of humanity. The terminal point of Marian devotion consists in the burning incense of adoration to God and the open hand to help the needy.

Marian devotion, solid in its foundations, beautiful and rich in its many expressions, open and transparent in its purpose, is not found in one person alone, nor in an institute of consecrated life, nor even in an entire people, but it flourishes within the universal Church, to which each particular church make its contribution.

CONCLUSION

77. Here it may be useful to once more formulate in a synthetic way the conclusions which have emerged in this letter on the qualities that theological reflection on the Mother of God should possess, as well as on the responsibilities and challenges facing Marian devotion on this dawn of Christianity's third millennium.

Our letter's only authority is derived from the convictions we have presented and from the Church's experience which they reflect. We hope that this letter offers suggestions and points of research to students of mariology who probably have already sensed the course we proposed for the future. Above all, mariology must be faithful to the historical and salvific context in vital contact with the Scriptures, and include the following qualities:

— *rigorous* in its use of sources, faithful in its methodological process, open to new approaches, such as the way of beauty, the experiential, theological narrative, and interdisciplinary studies;

— *relational* as it illuminates the intrinsic character of the bond uniting the Virgin Mary, who is totally relational, to God, Father, Son, and Holy Spirit; to Christ, eternal Wisdom become incarnate in her virginal womb; to the Church of which she is the outstanding and most eminent member; to the communion of saints in which she is lovingly and actively present; to humanity which she enhances by the perfection of her being, makes more radiant with her humility, and takes under her merciful protection on its journey toward the eschaton; to the cosmos because through her, in the event of the Incarnation of the Word, it has been changed by the divine gift of purification and transformation;

— *attentive to the liturgy* in which the experience of God becomes a source of theological knowledge, which transforms and reaches its culmination as a hymn of glory to God the Father for the great works which he has accomplished in Mary;

— *open to the values of popular piety* which have often been and continue to be the vehicle for the divine insights of the faithful (*sensus fidelium*);

— *imbued with a deep sense of belonging to the Church* by which 'the deep concerns of the Church' become one's own 'concerns,' such as the universal call to holiness, the purity of faith, the new evangelization, Christian unity, peace, the promotion of women, and the liberation of people from oppression;

— *ready to contribute* to the formation of a true Christian *ethical system* which addresses the moral questions of our time, and encourages Christians to serve generously the advancement of humanity;

— *affirming the historical reality* of Mary, the humble and poor woman of Israel, joined harmoniously to the *reality of grace* with which God favored her in view of her mission to be the Mother of Christ and the New Eve in the work of salvation;

— *reflecting the wondrous transcendence* of Mary, the creature completely immersed in the vision of God (cf. 1 Cor 13: 12), while closely united to the men and women of our time, who as mother and sister accompanies them on their journey of faith, in their sorrows and hopes;

— *leading toward an encounter* and a reciprocal influence including doctrinal research on the mission and person of Mary (*doctrina*), the unique devotion which the Church renders to her as the Theotokos and the all-holy one (*pietas*), and the *Marian inspiration* which assists the disciple to follow wholeheartedly the Lord and Master (*spiritualitas*);

— *preserving the memory* of our ancestors in faith, of the patriarchs and prophets, of the judges and kings, of the election of Israel and the covenant, of the great works accomplished by God in Mary (cf. Lk 1:49), of John the Baptist and Joseph of Nazareth, of the twelve apostles and of the primitive Church of Jerusalem (cf. Ac 1:12-15), and above all of the salvific events of Christ's life to which his mother was actively present; it is perception of the many ways in which Mary is *present* in the life of the Church as helper of the Christian people; it is a reflection on the Virgin's role, "until the day of the Lord shall come (cf. 2 P 3:10), as a sign of sure hope and solace to the people of God during its sojourn on earth."[296]

Mariology, theological discourse on Mary of Nazareth, has its beginnings in the plan of God, flows from and is absorbed in God. Mariology investigates revelation's source and looks on high toward the Virgin, and then it descends to the world to participate fully in its destiny. In the final analysis, mariology is doxology, "a ceaseless *Magnificat* of praise to the Father, to the Son, and to the Holy Spirit,"[297] and of compassionate love and service for all the world.

---

[296] *LG*, 68.
[297] John Paul II, "Renew Devotion to Mary, Mother of God," homily during the concelebration at the conclusion of the XX Mariological-Marian Congress (24 September 2000), 6, in *OR* (27 September 2000), 1.